Darren Callahan's
SCHOOLGIRL SWEETHEARTS

# Battery Filmtext

The Collected Screenplays of Darren Callahan
Limited Edition Series

Published in the United States of America by Battery Filmtext

Printed in the United States of America

Battery Filmtext and its logo are registered trademarks of
HCC Limited Release

Design, Materials, and Essay Content © Battery Filmtext, Norman Berklein
Battery Filmtext, Los Angeles, California, U.S.A.
www.batteryfilmtext.com

Screenplay © Darren Callahan, All Rights Reserved

The Library of Congress Catalog
Callahan, Darren
Collected Screenplays: Vol. 4: SCHOOLGIRL SWEETHEARTS
1st ed. in the United States of America
p. cm.

ISBN 9798664188301

BATTERY FILMTEXT
publishes screenplays
(both produced and unproduced)
that are compelling examples of
thoughtful genre writing. Our focus is on
horror, exploitation, and vintage suspense/thriller.

Our editions are typically part of a limited edition series focused on
a single screenwriter. We bring attention to the stories we admire,
regardless of whether that story or its author are well-known.

In keeping the text as close to the authoring experience as possible,
we publish our scripts in draft form, sometimes with flaws or
typos intact, and without scene numbers.
Should a published screenplay evolve with later drafts,
editions are republished.

SCHOOLGIRL SWEETHEARTS
is as dishonest as they come. It lulls you into thinking
it's just sexist titillation and then morphs into a legitimate
and compelling mystery (with all its street names lifted from
Dashiell Hammett's 1927 novel Red Harvest). Or, perhaps, this
isn't a mystery after all; it's a love story. After all, the story begins
when Debbie Harlow meets Teresa Galbo — two 17-year-olds leading
very separate, yet equally dangerous lives. Debbie Harlow is not that
different from other strong women in Callahan's works, excluding
the fact that she never sheds a tear, never breaks down, and, only
a few times, doubts her own abilities. Street smart, tenacious,
courageous, but also kind-hearted, she's a character who's hard
to let go. If only there were more Debbie Harlows in the world.

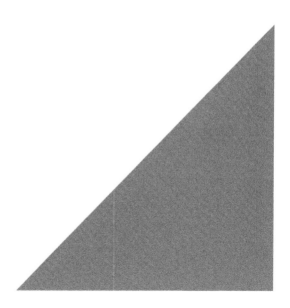

EXT. HIGH SCHOOL - FIELD - DAWN

There she sits.  Cross-legged on the grass.

DEBBIE HARLOW -- 17.  Dyed, unwashed hair.  Careless makeup.
Young, but not a child.  Denim jacket, terry cloth tank top,
ripped jeans, sneakers.  Zen calm or world weariness -- hard
to tell.

Smokes the last inch of an unfiltered cigarette.

Stamps it out in the grass.

She's under the goalpost of a practice field.

Ahead: a school shrouded in morning mist.

A distant bell rings.

Debbie lazily applies her lipstick.

Kisses the air.

Winds the straps of her bookbag into her fingers.

Stands, straightens.

With lazy swings of her bag, Debbie marches to school.

INT. HIGH SCHOOL - HALLWAY - DAY

Debbie enters the high school.

Posters promote the football team and the upcoming dance.

No one in the hallway.  Only chatter though doors.

She's late.

An ANNOUNCER echoes from the speakers pinned to the walls.

                    ANNOUNCER (O.S.)
          Good morning, Redmont High!  It is
          Tuesday, September 20th -- just
          four days until the homecoming game
          and just five days to the dance.
          Have you got your tickets yet?  If
          not, today at lunch..."

Announcements continue.

INT. HIGH SCHOOL - CENTRAL OFFICE - DAY

The high school's central office.

Authoritarian.  Institutional.

A FRUMPY MAN in an ill-fitting suit prepares paperwork.

Debbie's eyes set upon a girl leaned into the counter.

TERESA GALBO -- 17, lithe, straight red hair, striking features.

A look passes between the girls.

The Frumpy Man pushes a paper to Teresa.

>               FRUMPY MAN
>       Here you go, Miss Galbo.  Your
>       homeroom is 107 -- it's just down
>       the hall.  Follow this schedule
>       today and check back at the end of
>       day for your bus assignment.

>               TERESA
>       Got it.  Thanks.

>               FRUMPY MAN
>       To the left.

Teresa follows his point and exits.

>               FRUMPY MAN (CONT'D)
>           (disappointed)
>       Now... Miss Harlow.  I can't
>       imagine what you would need today.

He checks a ledger, stamps a slip of paper.

>               FRUMPY MAN (CONT'D)
>       Your late pass.

From around a corner:

>               WOMAN'S VOICE (O.S.)
>       Miss Harlow!

Debbie rolls her eyes.

PRINCIPAL GALE -- 50s, a woman -- behind a desk.

Debbie crosses the counter.  Sits.  A familiar ritual.

                    GALE
          We're only 20 days into the year.
          Do you really want to break last
          year's record?

                    DEBBIE
          I'm very competitive, Principal
          Gale.

ale leans back.

                    GALE
          If you're late one more time this
          semester, I'm going to have a
          problem with that.
                    (beat)
          Don't you care what happens to you,
          Debbie?

                    DEBBIE
          Oh, I care.

                    GALE
          You need to learn responsibility.
          You're not a little girl any more.


NT. HIGH SCHOOL - CLASSROOM - DAY

ebbie enters a class.

he TEACHER stops lecturing.

                    TEACHER
          Good morning, Miss Harlow.

ebbie hands over the late pass.

                    TEACHER (CONT'D)
          Page 31.

estures to a chair.

ebbie sits, opens a book.  Random page.  Pretends to
isten.

he surrounding STUDENTS stare at her and...

..one by one... look away.

EXT. HIGH SCHOOL - FIELD - DAY

End of day bell.

Debbie, once more, smokes under the goalpost.

A field hockey team scrimmages at the opposite end.

A young man spots her.

SEAN HALSEY -- 20s, athletic, gray sweat-shirt with a
whistle around his neck.  Makes his way to Debbie.

> SEAN
> I told you no smoking here.

> DEBBIE
> That was yesterday.

> SEAN
> Rule still stands.

> DEBBIE
> You're just a first-year.  I don't
> have to listen to you.

> SEAN
> Yes.  You do.

> DEBBIE
> Mr. Halsey-- or should I call you
> Sean?

> SEAN
> Mr. Halsey.

> DEBBIE
> All day long people tell me what to
> do.  Can't I have this one...
> little... cigarette?

> SEAN
> Not on school property.

Debbie takes a drag, gives an alluring look.

> SEAN (CONT'D)
> I'm gonna have to write you up.

> DEBBIE
> Do you smoke?

> SEAN
> Where do you get those?

> DEBBIE
> I steal 'em from my step-mom.

She takes another looong drag.

> SEAN
> Just... do it off school property.

Sean starts to walk away.

Debbie hasn't moved.  He turns.

> SEAN (CONT'D)
> You're gonna make me spank you.

She puts out her cigarette.

> DEBBIE
> Since you asked nice.

She rises, walks away.

Sean leers as she goes.

Back to the field hockey scrimmage.


EXT. PLAYGROUND - DUSK

Getting dark.

Debbie, on a swing in an empty playground.

Cigarette dangling.

Kicks her legs, swings high.

At the apex, notices:

The hedge that lines the playground.  Beyond -- a FIGURE glimpsed in the grass.  Small, seated.  Bare legs, no shoes.

Debbie slows her swing.  Stops.

Listens.

SOUND: a child's soft crying.

She jumps from the swing, rounds to the hedge.

There...

NAT -- 10, dark circles under the eyes and small frame.

Knees badly skinned, bleeding, in pain, weeping.

Debbie drops down beside.

>                    DEBBIE
>          Hello.
>               (beat)
>          That looks bad.  Did you fall?

>                    NAT
>          Two boys pushed me.

Debbie looks around.

>                    DEBBIE
>          And where are those boys now?

>                    NAT
>          They left.

>                    DEBBIE
>          Which direction?

Nat points.

>                    DEBBIE (CONT'D)
>          Older?

>                    NAT
>          Yes.

Debbie inspects Nat's wounds.  Raw.

>                    NAT (CONT'D)
>          Don't touch it!

The girl squirms.

>                    DEBBIE
>          What's your name?

>                    NAT
>          Nat.

>                    DEBBIE
>          Is that short for Natalie?

Nat nods.

>                    DEBBIE (CONT'D)
>          I'm Debbie.  Short for Deborah.
>          What grade are you in?

>                    NAT
>          Fifth.

>                    DEBBIE
>          Oh, wow.  Gettin' so grown up.  Can
>          you stand?  I'll get you home.

Debbie helps Nat to her feet, wipes the girl's eyes.

EXT. ALLEY - DAY

Debbie escorts Nat down an alleyway lined with garages.

The girl limps, but she's stopped crying.

>                    DEBBIE
>          I haven't seen you before.

>                    NAT
>          We just moved here.

>                    DEBBIE
>          Oh.  Where do you live?

>                    NAT
>          426 Noonan Street.

BANG! -- like a gunshot.

At the end of the alley:

TWO TEENAGE BOYS in fuzzy-collared jackets kick a crappy
soccer ball against a garage door.

>                    DEBBIE
>          Are those the boys who pushed you?

>                    NAT
>          Yes.

Nat starts to tear-up.

Debbie takes out a cigarette.  Lights it.

Gently, she guides Nat behind a fence.

                    DEBBIE
          Wait here, okay?

                    NAT
          What are you gonna do?

                    DEBBIE
          Don't watch.

Nat dries her eyes.

Debbie stuffs her hands in her pockets and makes her way to
the boys.  Within a few yards, the boys stop their goofing.

JASON KIRKPATRICK -- 17, thick, ragged, stooped.

KELLY KIRKPATRICK -- 16, wiry, buzz-cut, same genes.

Debbie stays silent.  Inserts between the two.  Picks up the
soccer ball.

                    JASON
          Hey -- that ball was in the trash.
          We didn't take it.

                    DEBBIE
          You brothers?

                    JASON
          Yeah.

                    DEBBIE
          Go to Redmont?

                    JASON
          No.  Vocational.

Jason lifts the ball from Debbie, smiles.

Tosses the ball over his shoulder.

                    JASON (CONT'D)
               (re: cigarette)
          Give me one of those.

Debbie taps one from her pack, hands it over.

                    JASON (CONT'D)
          Got a light?

With her Bic, she lights for him.

                    JASON (CONT'D)
          You look like fun.

                    DEBBIE
          I am fun.

                    JASON
          We like fun.  We got some whiskey.
          And a car.

                    DEBBIE
          Oh.  Do you.

                    KELLY
          Yeah, it's just--

e hooks a finger to a random nowhere.

                    DEBBIE
          Where you devils live?

                    KELLY
          Reno Street.

                    DEBBIE
          Ooo, that IS close.  What should I
          call you?

                    JASON
          Jason.  Kelly.  The Kirkpatrick
          brothers.  And you, sexy pants?

                    DEBBIE
          Debbie Harlow.

                    JASON
          Sounds real slutty.

e takes a drag on the cigarette.

                    DEBBIE
          Hey.  Just curious.  Did you push
          some stupid little girl?

                    JASON
          Huh?

                    DEBBIE
          Back at the playground.

son -- a huff.

                    JASON
          Who you been talkin' to?

                    DEBBIE
          No one.  I saw it.

                    JASON
          You saw us do that?  Like a half
          hour ago?

                    DEBBIE
          Yeah.

Jason flicks ash from his cigarette.

                    JASON
          So, what do you say, Debs?  You
          want to come back to our house and
          party or wh-?

--POW!

Debbie's fist connects with Jason's jaw.

He goes down fast.

She presses her advantage -- kicks, pounds.

Kelly tries to YANK her off his brother, but she shakes him
loose, keeps wailing on Jason.

Kelly finally gets a grip, but she bends, rams back into
him, knocks him flat.  He hits his head -- hard.

She's up and kicking.

Jason rolls in pain.

Kelly tightens into a ball.

                    KELLY
          Stop!  Stop!

She slows.  Breathes.

Breathes.

Breathes.

Both boys are hurt bad.  Writhing on the gravel.

She drops a fresh cigarette on Jason.

nother on his brother.

>           DEBBIE
>      Smoke these when the swelling goes
>      down.  And don't let me catch you
>      hurting any little kids again.

he returns to the fence.

at, tucked away.

ebbie gently takes the younger girl's hand.

>           DEBBIE (CONT'D)
>      You see any of that?

>           NAT

>      Yes.

>           DEBBIE
>      Sorry.  I had to.

ebbie leads Nat out of the alley.

at -- a curled smile.


XT. SPLIT-LEVEL HOME - DUSK

un's down.

n the porch of a simple brick split-level home, Debbie
ifts Nat to the stoop then slips under the shadow of a
ree.

efore the girl is able to get inside--

-the door SWINGS open!

here stands Teresa Galbo.

rom the central office that morning, now in pajamas.

t first, she acknowledges only Nat.

>           TERESA
>      Where the hell have you been!

otices Nat's wounds.

>           TERESA (CONT'D)
>      Oh, no.  What did you do?

                        NAT
          I fell.

Teresa spots Debbie.

                        TERESA
          Who are you?

                        DEBBIE
          I just walked her home.  She fell
          off a swing.

                        TERESA
          Oh.
                (to Nat)
          Into the bathroom.  I'll wash it
          out.

Debbie turns to leave.

                        TERESA (CONT'D)
          Hey!

Meets eyes.

                        TERESA (CONT'D)
          Thanks.

Debbie nods, then splits, hands in pockets.


INT. RANCH HOUSE - LIVING ROOM - NIGHT

A lousy ranch house -- poorly kept, cheap furniture, peelin
paint, tiny rooms.

In the center, a La-Z-Boy chair.

Slumped in it:

COLE HARLOW -- 40s.  Mechanic overalls, bushy beard, floppy
hair.  Snores.  In his hand: a smoldering tobacco pipe.

Debbie enters quietly.

Steps to Cole.  Lifts the pipe and sets it in a standing
ashtray.  Doesn't wake him.

From the kitchen arch:

BRENDA HARLOW -- 50s, stringy, holds a dirty paper plate.

>                    BRENDA
>           Finally.

>                    DEBBIE
>           Shhh.  He's asleep.

>                    BRENDA
>           It's nearly 10.

ebbie burrows past Brenda and--

NT. RANCH HOUSE - KITCHEN - NIGHT

-into the ranch house's kitchen.

ebbie keeps her voice low; Brenda doesn't.

>                    DEBBIE
>           Have you been smoking my goddamn
>           cigarettes?

ebbie fills a paper cup with tap water.

>                    BRENDA
>           What happened to your hand?

nuckles bloody.

>                    DEBBIE
>               (re: blood)
>           Don't worry.  It's not my blood.

ne crushes the cup, tosses it, washes the blood in the
ink.

>                    BRENDA
>           You shouldn't be fighting.

>                    DEBBIE
>               (resigned)
>           Well I don't like it either.

ause.

>                    BRENDA
>           Did you eat?

>                    DEBBIE
>           No, I guess I didn't.

> BRENDA
>
> I can make a turkey sandwich.

> DEBBIE
>
> Sure.

Brenda makes the food.

Debbie slumps at the table.

> BRENDA
>
> The school called.

> DEBBIE
>
> I missed the bus.

When finished, Brenda sets a paper plate with a simple sandwich in front of Debbie, who eats.

> BRENDA
>
> We bought you a clock.  You can't just keep hitting the snooze button.

> DEBBIE
>
> I know!

Debbie eats.

> BRENDA
>
> I'm goin' to bed.

Brenda exits the kitchen.

Debbie finishes her sandwich in silence.


INT. RANCH HOUSE - BEDROOM - DAY

Debbie, in sloppy sheets, center of a crowded bedroom fille
with stuffed toys and rock posters.

The alarm SOUNDS.

Debbie hits 'snooze.'

After a moment, her eyes slowly open.

Makes note of the time on the clock.

Springs out of bed!

                    DEBBIE
          Fuck me!

INT. HIGH SCHOOL - HALLWAY - DAY

Same as the day before.  Late.  Again.

Debbie enters the vacant halls of Redmont High.

INT. HIGH SCHOOL - CENTRAL OFFICE - DAY

Debbie slips in the open door of the central office.

The Frumpy Man, back turned -- only one present.

Debbie sneaks along the wall.

Reaches over the counter.

Lifts a tardy slip from the stack.

Stamps it.

The Frumpy Man, about to turn...

...but doesn't.

Debbie backs out, unseen.

INT. HIGH SCHOOL - LUNCHROOM - DAY

The school's packed lunchroom.

Debbie eats alone.

Teresa, with lunch tray, plunks down beside.

                    TERESA
          Hi.

                    DEBBIE
          Hello.

                    TERESA
          Thanks again for bringing Nat home.

                    DEBBIE
          Yep.

                    TERESA
          She confessed.

Debbie sips her milk, raises her brow.

                    TERESA (CONT'D)
          I don't like her seeing things like
          that.  Even if it was--

                    DEBBIE
          --I told her not to watch.  If it
          makes you feel better, those
          fuckers won't push another kid off
          a swing without thinking twice.

                    TERESA
          Do you fight a lot?  She said you
          were pretty great.

                    DEBBIE
          I used to.  But then I found Jesus.

                    TERESA
          Really?

                    DEBBIE
          No.

She drinks more milk.

                    TERESA
          My father runs a church.  Don't
          worry.  We're not, like, crazy
          Christians or anything.  You know
          those storefronts on MacSwain?  He
          rents one of them.  It's not fancy.
          The Church of New Light.  Do you
          know it?

Debbie shakes her head.

                    TERESA (CONT'D)
          I help out after school.  Stop by
          if you want.

                    DEBBIE
          I don't really want to find Jesus.

                    TERESA
          Just come and hang out.

                    DEBBIE
          I appreciate the invitation.  But I
          probably won't.

                    TERESA
          We get donations all the time.  All
          kinds of stuff.  Do you want some
          clothes?  Some cute tops and--

                    DEBBIE
          --I'm good.

ause.  Teresa stands.

                    TERESA
          Okay.  See you.

eresa, with her tray, leaves with a smile.  Moves a few
ables over.  Sits.  Starts up a conversation with OTHER
TUDENTS.

lone, Debbie finishes her milk.  Crushes the box.

                                        DISSOLVE TO:


XT. FOOTBALL FIELD - NIGHT

ame night.

he Redmont Redbirds versus their rivals.

acked bleachers and bright lights that cut the autumn
ight.

ARENTS and STUDENTS.

 GAME ANNOUNCER over a PA.

HEERLEADERS kick and flip.

ig-shouldered PLAYERS take the field.

EPPY STUDENTS rise and fall to get a "wave" going.

 luck.

EVEAL:

ebbie Harlow -- against the lower rail, denim jacket and
ort shorts.

Rolls her eyes, turns opposite and--

--slips under the bleachers--

--into a clutch of STUDENTS who sneak kisses and cigarettes.

Debbie moves to light one of her own, but stops.

A SECURITY GUARD sweeps with a flashlight.

Catches a GIRL with her hands down a BOY's pants.

                    SECURITY GUARD
          Not here, guys.  Not here.

The teens scurry like cockroaches.

Debbie remains in shadow.

Waits until the Security Guard moves along.

At last, she lights up.

Tucked even further under the bleachers--

--BRAYDON WYATT.

Only 15 years old, chubby, ripped rock tee and jeans.

                    BRAYDON
          Hey there, Deb.

Debbie turns.

                    DEBBIE
          I thought I was alone.

                    BRAYDON
          Can I borrow your lighter?

Debbie slips next to Braydon.  Hands over her Bic.

In his hand: a marijuana one-hitter.

He lights, takes a long drag.  As he holds in the smoke--

                    BRAYDON (CONT'D)
          --Thanks.

                    DEBBIE
          I haven't seen you since summer
          school.

                    BRAYDON
          I was downstate.

                    DEBBIE
          Reform school again?

                    BRAYDON
          Can't say or I'd have to kill you.

e re-packs and offers her the one-hitter.

                    DEBBIE
          I'm afraid of germs.

                    BRAYDON
          The bud kills germs dead.

he wipes the pipe and takes a hit.  Hands it back.

                    DEBBIE
          I thought you hated football.

                    BRAYDON
          But I love the sound of a cheering
          crowd.  How're things?

                    DEBBIE
          Things.  Well they're the same as
          always, aren't they?  What are you
          up to?

                    BRAYDON
          I got a job.

                    DEBBIE
          Someone paying the notorious
          Braydon Wyatt to steal cars again?

                    BRAYDON
          That was last year's gig.  Now I'm
          working for a big timer.

                    DEBBIE
          Sounds dangerous.

e takes another hit and holds.

                    BRAYDON
          If it gets too fucked up, I'll
          bail.

                    DEBBIE
          Someone from Redmont?

                    BRAYDON
          You don't know 'im.

He clams up.  Hands back her lighter.

                         BRAYDON (CONT'D)
               Thanks.

Debbie stands.

                    DEBBIE
          Don't get shot.

                    BRAYDON
          Enjoy the game.
                    (soft, fake cheer)
          Raaaahhhw.

                    DEBBIE
          I always enjoy the game.

She's gone.


EXT. SCHOOL GROUNDS - NIGHT - LATER

Distant, the football game continues -- sound and splendor
bleed into the school grounds.

STUDENTS roam the quad.

Among them, Debbie, who keeps to herself.

Catches sight of:

Sean Halsey.

He flirts with FEMALE STUDENTS near the school's entrance.

Debbie takes out her phone.

She snaps a picture of the teacher with the students.

Keeps moving.

Around another corner, she finds a window, hidden by a
hedge.

She presses her hand to the glass.

nside, the school's basement--

                         TERESA (O.S.)
              --Whatcha doin'?

-Debbie startles-!

-Teresa hovers over the hedge.

                         DEBBIE
              Fuck me.  What are you doing here?
              Are you stalking me?  Don't you
              have to go to church or something?

ebbie takes Teresa by the arm, drags her around the hedge.

                         DEBBIE (CONT'D)
              Get down.

                         TERESA
              Why?

                         DEBBIE
              Because this is secret.

                         TERESA
              Ooooh, I like secrets.

ebbie continues top move along the windows.  Finds a spot.

MACKS the corner of a window and it POPS inward.

eaches in, flips a handle.

                         TERESA (CONT'D)
              You'll set off the alarm!

                         DEBBIE
              They stopped paying the ADT bill
              last year.  Budget cuts.

ebbie lifts a leg inside.

ets her foot on a desk beneath the window.

asses through.

w inside the basement:

                         DEBBIE (CONT'D)
              You comin'?

                    TERESA
          What!  No.

                    DEBBIE
          I'll help you down.

Long pause.

                    DEBBIE (CONT'D)
          Come on, coward.  I thought you
          like secrets.

Teresa puts a leg in.

Debbie guides her.


INT. HIGH SCHOOL - BASEMENT - NIGHT

The basement -- lit by moonlight.  Storage.  Boxes and
blackboards, cabinets and dust.

Debbie leads to a corner.

Sink and a small refrigerator.

Debbie opens the fridge.

The inner light -- bright in the dark.

Inside the fridge: a SIX PACK of beer.

Debbie lifts out the ring, leaves the door cracked.

Snaps a beer from the ring, pops the tab.  Drinks.  Offers
to Teresa, who breaks one off.

                    TERESA
          Whose is this?

                    DEBBIE
          Rick's.  The janitor.  He hides it.

                    TERESA
          How do you know so much?

                    DEBBIE
          My dad likes to call me "super
          fucking nosy."  One day, Rick came
          down here and I followed him.

Debbie drinks.  Fast.  Pops another.

>                         TERESA
>           Won't he freak if he finds all his
>           beer gone?

ebbie shrugs.  Doesn't care.

>                         TERESA (CONT'D)
>           I don't even know your name.

>                         DEBBIE
>           Debbie Harlow.  Girl about town.

links her can with Teresa's.

>                         TERESA
>           I'm Teresa Galbo.

eresa drinks.

>                         DEBBIE
>           Sorry I've been a bitch.

>                         TERESA
>           You're not a--

>                         DEBBIE
>           --So are you stalking me?

>                         TERESA
>           The enemy of my enemy is my friend.

>                         DEBBIE
>           I just hate bullies.  Plus, we're
>           17.  We're supposed to be angry.

ing!  A text on a Teresa's phone.

>                         TERESA
>           My dad.

>                         DEBBIE
>           Guess you better answer.

ebbie cracks another beer.

>                         TERESA
>           I'll just tell him I'm fine.

he texts.  Sends.  Pockets the phone.

> DEBBIE
> Did you mention you were drinking
> with THE Debbie Harlow?

Ding!  Another message.  Teresa reads.

> TERESA
> He wants to know the score.

> DEBBIE
> Just say we're losing.  You don't
> know this yet, but we always lose.

Teresa texts her father.

> TERESA
> What if he asks for the actual
> number?

> DEBBIE
> I guess you better go back and
> watch the game.

> TERESA
> My dad's so protective.  He's
> always like this when I switch
> schools.

> DEBBIE
> So you switch a lot?

Teresa nods.

> DEBBIE (CONT'D)
> What about your mom?

> TERESA
> Left three months ago.  Woke up and
> she was gone.  Not sure where she
> is.  You?

> DEBBIE
> My dad remarried.

> TERESA
> How's that going?

> DEBBIE
>         (laughs)
> Like you'd expect.  Brenda thinks
> she's my mom.  Some days she's
>                 (MORE)

                    DEBBIE(CONT'D)
          okay.  My dad's a mechanic at
          Sim's.  Near the overpass.  If your
          car breaks down, call me.

                    TERESA
          I don't have a car.

                    DEBBIE
          Me either.  My license was
          suspended anyway.  Speeding.  Lots
          of speeding.

hey drink.

                    TERESA
          I should get back to the game.

he hands over the empty can.  Debbie crushes it.

                    DEBBIE
          Going to homecoming?

                    TERESA
          I don't have a date.

                    DEBBIE
          Lots of people go without dates.  I
          figured you don't know anyone yet.
          Text me if you show up.  I was
          gonna go.  You can learn a lot at a
          dance.

ebbie holds out her phone's screen.

                    DEBBIE (CONT'D)
          Here's my number.

eresa enters Debbie's number into her phone.

                    TERESA
          Thanks.

vkward smile between them.

                                        CUT TO:

ebbie helps Teresa out the basement window.

1en out--

>               TERESA (CONT'D)
>     Do you want me to help you up?

>               DEBBIE
>     No way.  I got beers to drink!

>               TERESA
>     I bet.  Don't get busted.

With a wave, she's gone.


INT. HIGH SCHOOL - HALLWAY - NIGHT - LATER

Debbie carries the last beer.  It hangs off the six-pack.

She trespasses the dim halls of Redmont High.

Finds the central office.  Locked.

From her jacket, pulls out a compact.

Instead of makeup: mini-screwdrivers.

Using the light from her phone, Debbie picks the lock.


INT. HIGH SCHOOL - CENTRAL OFFICE - NIGHT

Inside the office, Debbie sets the beer on the counter.

Ducks under the brace, flips through files, phone as a
flashlight.

Folder label:

"LOCKER ASSIGNMENTS"


INT. HIGH SCHOOL - LOCKER BAY - NIGHT

Debbie counts the lockers.  Finds it.  #237.

With her screwdrivers, easily pops the lock.

Inside: books, folders.

On the door, a picture.

Teresa with Nat and an OLDER MAN, his arms around the two.

Debbie takes paper and pen from the locker, scrawls a note.

ets the last unopened beer, still in its ring, inside
eresa's locker.

From Rick the Janitor"

ith a smiley face.

leased, she shuts the locker, spins the combo lock.

NT. RANCH HOUSE - BEDROOM - DAY

ebbie, in clothes from the night before, wakes to:

OICES (O.S.): parents arguing.

mothers into her pillow.

NT. RANCH HOUSE - BATHROOM - DAY

fter a shower, Debbie, towel around her middle, puts on her
akeup.  Badly.  Shakes out her wet hair.

rops the towel and throws on a sweater and skirt.

XT. STOREFRONT CHURCH - DAY

uiet sunny day.

ebbie waits on a street corner.

n her sights: a curtained storefront.

o church artifacts or advertisements.  No people.

he building is next to a DRUG STORE.

he street sign.

MACSWAIN"

ebbie crosses the intersection.

ucked, nearly invisible, in the window is a poorly-printed
lacard:

THE CHURCH OF NEW LIFE"

he tries the door.  Locked.

Suddenly-!

--the ROAR of a U-Haul truck!

It plows down the alley between the church and drug store.

Debbie rounds to look.

The truck stops next to the church's service door.

A HEAVY MAN with a lumberjack beard leaps from the driver's
seat, leaves the truck idling.  Comes around the rear door.
Snaps a padlock from the tail.

Debbie slips out of sight.

When she looks again -- the truck is there, but the Heavy
Man is...

...gone.

ZOOM TO:

Debbie returns to the front of the church.

Tries the main door again.

Won't open.

She drifts away, down MacSwain.


INT. SIM'S GARAGE - DAY

Debbie enters Sim's Garage -- a greasy repair shop.  Cars o:
lifts.  Country music buried by the clang of wrenches.

Cole Harlow -- her father -- on a creeper seat underneath a
jacked-up car.

Debbie waits by his feet.

When he rolls out--

                    COLE
          --Oh!  Heya, baby doll.

                    DEBBIE
          Thought I'd visit.

                    COLE
          That's... surprising.

ets up from the creeper.  Wipes his hands.

                    DEBBIE
          What were you and Brenda fighting
          about this morning?

                    COLE
          Who the hell knows?
               (beat)
          Have you eaten?

NT. SIM'S GARAGE - OFFICE - DAY

ebbie and her father, in the tight office of the garage.
e eats a sandwich.  She poaches his chips, playfully taps
he keys of the cash register.

                    COLE
          You going to the dance?

                    DEBBIE
          Probably.

                    COLE
          Got a date?

                    DEBBIE
          Ha.

                    COLE
          Get one.  But not an asshole.

                    DEBBIE
          I would never date an asshole, Dad.
               (beat)
          Hey, do you know anything about
          that new church on MacSwain?  Next
          to the drug store.

                    COLE
          Those are bullshit.  Why you ask?

                    DEBBIE
          Girl at school.  Her dad is the
          pastor or something.

                    COLE
          What do I know, baby doll?  I can
          barely figure out the transmission
          of that Chevy.

                    DEBBIE
          You can fix anything.

Cole touches his daughter's chin.

                    COLE
          That's not true.  And you know it.

She eats another chip.

Resigned, he surrenders his sandwich, too.


EXT. STOREFRONT CHURCH - DAY

Debbie returns to the church.  Still quiet.

Peers down the alley.  Truck gone.

Approaches the front door.  Pulls the handle.

This time, it opens!


INT. STOREFRONT CHURCH - MAIN ROOM - DAY

Inside The Church of New Life.

Low rent.  Musty.  Two dozen plastic chairs, a small altar,
a cross shrouded by dusty light.

Debbie holds in the center aisle.

Entering from a curtained side room--

TRENT GALBO -- mid-50s, wavy gray hair, in a slim-fit suit
with a loose necktie.  (He is the Older Man from the pictur
in Teresa's locker.)

Doesn't notice Debbie.

Digs in a candle box, draws out a few votives, continues to
search for something.

Debbie coughs.

                    GALBO
          Oh!  Good afternoon.  May I help
          you?

                    DEBBIE
          It wasn't locked.

                    GALBO
          That's okay.  Everyone is welcome.

                    DEBBIE
          Is Teresa Galbo here?

                    GALBO
          ...Who are you?

                    DEBBIE
          I'm from school.  She said
          something about clothes.

                    GALBO
          Oh.  Well.  Teresa's earning her
          allowance.  Let's walk back.

INT. STOREFRONT CHURCH - SORTING AREA - DAY

Galbo leads Debbie to a sorting area.

Stacked boxes by a service door.

On the floor, Teresa buried among piles of crumpled clothes.

                    GALBO
          Teresa.

The girl turns.  Smiles.

                    TERESA
          Hey!

                    DEBBIE
          Hey.

                    TERESA
          Wanna help?

                    GALBO
          I'll let you girls get to work.

Galbo exits with a smile.

                    DEBBIE
          That your dad?

                    TERESA
          Yep.  You don't really have to
          help.  I thought I was supposed to
          text you.

                    DEBBIE
          Decided to take you up on your
          offer of something to wear.  I
          don't own a lot of clothes.

                    TERESA
          Um, there might be some dresses.
          Dig if you want.  Boys there...
          Girls here.  Throw out anything
          ripped or ratty.  Pretty simple.

Teresa tosses a large brassiere to Debbie.

                    DEBBIE
          Is this ratty?

                    TERESA
          Try it on and see.

Debbie holds it up.  Comically big.

                    DEBBIE
          I don't think it's my size.

Teresa thumbs to the pile.

Debbie chucks the brassiere.

                    TERESA
          See?  Simple.

Teresa keeps sorting.

                    DEBBIE
          Do you get a lot of donations?

                    TERESA
          There's some pretty nice stuff
          sometimes.

Debbie eyes the stock.  Finds a mini-skirt.

                    TERESA (CONT'D)
          Try it on.

Debbie holds it to her body.

                    DEBBIE
          Looks short.

                    TERESA
          Go ahead.  I won't peek.

ebbie hesitates.  Checks over her shoulder.  Slips out of
er longer skirt and tries on the mini-skirt.  Teresa does,
n fact, peek.

>                    DEBBIE
>          How is it?

>                    TERESA
>          Criminal.

>                    DEBBIE
>          Probably too cold for the dance
>          anyway.

>                    TERESA
>          Keep it for summer then.  I'm sure
>          there's more in here.

ebbie presses the skirt to her body.  Likes it.

                                        DISSOLVE TO:

NT. STOREFRONT CHURCH - SORTING AREA - DAY - LATER

eresa and Debbie try on more clothes.

njoying.

 look in their eyes.  Something charges the room.

hen Teresa takes off her sweater to try on a baseball tee,
ebbie notices her simple white bra underneath.

nd Teresa notices Debbie taking notice.

>                    TERESA
>          About tonight.  Would it be weird
>          if we show up together?

>                    DEBBIE
>          Some kids show up together even if
>          they aren't a couple.

>                    TERESA
>          Yeah, but would that be... weird?

>                    DEBBIE
>          People know me.

>                    TERESA
>          What do you mean?

                    DEBBIE
          I cause trouble.

                    TERESA
          Oh, I know.

Teresa considers.

                    TERESA (CONT'D)
          Okay.  Let's do it.


INT. HIGH SCHOOL - GYM - DAY

The homecoming dance raves on in the Redmont High gymnasium.

A hundred Students.  Dance floor.  Too-loud DJ.

Bleachers, flanked by TEACHERS.

Some Students are noticeably drunk, others kiss in dark pockets of the gym.

Entering--

--Debbie.

60s-style black dress with a white collar.

Hair and makeup without effort, but still striking.

Teresa wears a knit sweater with long sleeves and short hem.

                    DEBBIE
          You ready for this?

                    TERESA
          We should be drunk.

                    DEBBIE
          You're the craziest preacher's
          daughter I've ever met.

Teresa smiles.  The girls enter the fray.

Teresa dances with a NERDY BOY to a fast-tempo song.

From the bleachers, Debbie watches, sips punch.  Smiles.

Teresa's dancing isn't great, but charming nonetheless.  The
Nerdy Boy tries out all sorts of moves (none of them good).
But Teresa laughs with him, not at him.

hen the song is over, breathless, Teresa finds Debbie on
he bleachers.

                 DEBBIE (CONT'D)
Timothy.

                 TERESA
      (not hearing)
What?

                 DEBBIE
That's his name.

                 TERESA
Oh.  You know him?

                 DEBBIE
Nope.

                 TERESA
Then how do you know his name?

                 DEBBIE
Look -- I should tell you this.
I am really good with finding
things out.

                 TERESA
Like if there's beer in the
basement?

                 DEBBIE
Yeah.  That.

                 TERESA
What else are you good at?

                 DEBBIE
Fuckin' up.

                 TERESA
You're trouble... you fuck up.  I'm
beginning to think I picked the
wrong girl to be my friend.

                 DEBBIE
YOU picked ME?

                 TERESA
Of course.  Don't worry -- I don't
care if you're fucked-up trouble.

Teresa looks out at the dance floor.

>                    TERESA (CONT'D)
>           You ever dance?

>                    DEBBIE
>           I don't like to get sweaty.

>                    TERESA
>           Dance with me.

>                    DEBBIE
>                (dry)
>           But I don't wanna get sweaty.

>                    TERESA
>           I don't mind sweat.  I mind you
>           going to a dance and not dancing!

Teresa drags Debbie to the floor.

A new song starts.

They dance.  Silly at first.  Then.  Carelessly.
Alluringly.  Like no one's watching.  People are.  It's
infectious.

Soon they are in a mass of Students, bopping up and down.

Happy.

>                                        DISSOLVE TO:


EXT. STREET - NIGHT

Debbie and Teresa, after the dance.

Stroll under a lamp-lit street, alone.

Crickets and night sounds, distant cars.

>                    TERESA
>           I love fall.

>                    DEBBIE
>           You move a lot with your dad?

>                    TERESA
>           It's like he's on the run.

                    DEBBIE
          Is he?

                    TERESA
          Just reassignments.

                    DEBBIE
          How about Nat?

                    TERESA
          She hates it.  Has to make new
          friends all the time.  At least
          she's got me.

Debbie lights a cigarette.  Offers one to Teresa, who
accepts.

They turn a corner.

MacSwain.  The storefront church.

As they pass, Teresa waves.

                    TERESA (CONT'D)
          Hello, Church of New Life!

                    DEBBIE
          What is that, like, Lutheran or
          something?

                    TERESA
          I don't know.

                    DEBBIE
          You don't have to go on Sundays?

                    TERESA
          Never.

EXT. SPLIT-LEVEL HOME - NIGHT

Debbie and Teresa arrive outside Teresa's house.  Moon over
the street, porch light on.

                    TERESA
          Thanks for being my date.

                    DEBBIE
          Thanks for making me dance.

Teresa comes in close, touches Debbie's face.

                    TERESA
          See?  Not that sweaty.

She holds (a little long).

                    DEBBIE
          So.  When you gonna leave Redmont?
          I feel like we just met.

                    TERESA
          If I disappear, just say to
          yourself, "She's just on vacation."
          She'll come back to me.

Awkward space between.

                    TERESA (CONT'D)
          Stop by the church tomorrow, if you
          want.  We got a few more boxes.
          Maybe there's something cool.

                    DEBBIE
          Okay.  Bye.

                    TERESA
          See you.

Teresa departs with a caress of Debbie's arm.


INT. RANCH HOUSE - LIVING ROOM - DAY

Debbie quietly enters her house.

Cole -- asleep in his La-Z-Boy.

Debbie once more lifts the spent pipe from his hand.


INT. RANCH HOUSE - BEDROOM - DAY

Debbie, in her bed in the dark.  Wide awake.  Smiles.

                                        DISSOLVE TO:


EXT. STOREFRONT CHURCH - DAY

Debbie -- tee shirt, black hoodie, blue jeans.  Beautiful
autumn day, with birds and bright sun.

Passes the drug store, then the alley.

uts on the brakes.

POV:
The U-Haul -- once more by the service door.

BANG!

--The church door CRASHES open and--

--TWO MEN--

--The Heavy Man, from before, along with a PUDGY MAN -- also
ith a lumberjack beard.

he men struggle with a zippered, oblong bag.

he Heavy Man racks open the rear door of the truck.  Empty
nside.  They toss the bag into the container.

uddenly-!

--the top zipper of the bag splits open!

nside--

--Teresa!  Mouth taped, hands tied.

he Pudgy Man climbs into the U-Haul.

hoves Teresa backwards and re-zips the bag.

ebbie rushes forward!

                    DEBBIE
          Hey, you fucks!

he men don't acknowledge her.

he Heavy Man slams the door, seals Teresa inside with the
udgy Man.

ebbie races for the truck.

                    DEBBIE (CONT'D)
          Hey!  Stop!  Hey!

he Heavy Man hops behind the wheel and--

                    DEBBIE (CONT'D)
          Stop!

--the truck ROCKETS out of the other side of the alley--

EXT. STREET - DAY - CONTINUOUS

--Debbie CHASES the truck down the street.

Nearly reaches it -- hand out to the bumper.

Truck hits a curb, takes a hard turn, barrels away.

Debbie will never catch it.

Slows and stops.  Stands huffing.

BRAKES scream-!

--ANOTHER CAR nearly strikes Debbie in the road!

The DRIVER leans out his window.

                    DRIVER
          Get outta the fucking road!

Debbie keeps her cool.

                    DEBBIE
          That truck took my friend!

Debbie whips out her phone.

                    DRIVER
          What?  What did you say?

Debbie's eyes: panic.


INT. POLICE STATION - OFFICE - DAY

Debbie, seen through an inner office window.

DETECTIVES and UNIFORMED OFFICERS surround.

Words, no sound.

                                        DISSOLVE TO:


INT. POLICE STATION - WAITING AREA - DAY

Debbie exits the police station office, walks to a waiting
area.  In chairs: Trent Galbo, with Nat in his arms.

Galbo hops up, anxious for news.

                         GALBO
          Did you-?

                         DEBBIE
          --I told them everything.

at starts to cry.  Galbo comforts her.

 UNIFORMED OFFICER signals for Galbo.

                         GALBO
          Can you stay with Nat?  I don't
          want her to be alone.

                         DEBBIE
          Sure.

albo moves into the office and the door shuts.

ebbie sits next to Nat.

at folds into Debbie.

                         DEBBIE (CONT'D)
          Someone'll find her.

er face is not so certain.


NT. RANCH HOUSE - BATHROOM - DAY

ebbie stares into her bathroom mirror.

rags on a cigarette.

 knock.

                         DEBBIE
          Go away!

                         BRENDA (O.S.)
          Don't talk to me like that.
               (beat)
          Are you smoking my cigarettes?

                         DEBBIE
          Go away!

                         BRENDA
          ...You should eat your dinner.

                    DEBBIE
               (softer)
          ...Go away.


INT. RANCH HOUSE - BEDROOM - DUSK

In the orange light from her window, Debbie sits on her bed
in tee shirt and pajama pants.

The door opens.

Cole Harlow casts a shadow.

                    COLE
               (half-joking)
          Why you being a bitch?

Cole sits next to her.

                    COLE (CONT'D)
          Did you get into trouble again?

                    DEBBIE
          No.

                    COLE
          Well.  That's good, I s'pose.  So.
          What?

                    DEBBIE
          A girl from school got kidnapped.

                    COLE
          Shit.  Really?  Did you know her?

                    DEBBIE
          I did but I didn't.  We just
          started hanging out.

                    COLE
          They know who did it?

She shakes her head.

A distant telephone rings.

                    COLE (CONT'D)
          Brenda'll get that.

                    DEBBIE
          That's the police.

he ringing stops.

                    BRENDA (O.S.)
          Hello?

                    COLE
          The police?  Deborah Lynn.  What's
          going on?

                    DEBBIE
          I saw it happen.  The police said
          they'd call tonight.  They want to
          talk to you.

                    BRENDA (O.S.)
          Cole, I need you here!  Now!

ole stands.

                    COLE
          Stay put.

e exits.

OUND (O.S.): voices.

ebbie slips from her bed, throws on shoes and a jacket.

ifts her bedroom window--

XT. RANCH HOUSE - DUSK - CONTINUOUS

-Debbie drops onto the lawn from her window.

lips away into the dusk.

NT. HIGH SCHOOL - LOCKER BAY - DAY

he locker boy.  KIDS disperse.  The bell rings.

ebbie is left alone in the bay.  Late for class.

he passes locker #237.  Cracks it.

nside: the gifted beer on its plastic ring.  Lonely.

ebbie stares at the can a long time.

akes it out.

Pops the top, downs it.  Crushes the can.

Tosses the empty back inside the locker.


EXT. HIGH SCHOOL - DAY

Debbie escapes the school, undetected.


EXT. STOREFRONT CHURCH - DAY

Debbie arrives on MacSwain Street, at The Church of New
Life.  Tries the door.  Locked.

A note has been taped inside the door:

"BACK THIS SUNDAY"

She moves to the service door.

Tries the handle.  Locked.

Spots a trash dumpster.

Lifts the lid--

                    OLD MAN (O.S.)
          --Fuck you doin'-?

--Debbie drops the lid.

An OLD MAN in ragged clothes.  Along a brick wall.  Pants
down.

                    DEBBIE
          What are YOU doing?

                    OLD MAN
          Takin' a piss.

                    DEBBIE
          You piss here a lot?

No answer.  He lets his stream go.

                    DEBBIE (CONT'D)
          A girl was kidnapped yesterday, in
          this alley.

                    OLD MAN
          If you're looking for her in the
          garbage, don't bother.  They
          checked there.

                    DEBBIE
          The cops checked the dumpster?

                    OLD MAN
          The lid was open.  And rats don't
          have the strength.

                    DEBBIE
          What if someone else looked in
          there?

inished, he zips.

                    OLD MAN
          What -- like those two brothers?
          Come here every coupla days.

XT. STREET - DAY

ebbie walks another small town street.

heap row houses.

ign: "RENO STREET"

he passes by the alley of garages -- from the Kirkpatrick's
nd their stolen soccer ball.

t the junction, she waits.  Hidden by a wall.

ights a cigarette.  Smokes.  All cool.  Patient.

                              DISSOLVE TO:

ebbie, same spot.  Pile of cigarette butts at her feet.

here-!

-Jason and Kelly Kirkpatrick walk down the alley onto Reno.

ebbie's tracks them to a nearby house.

hey're not inside a few seconds when--

-the brothers STORM back out, hop into a blue Chevy Impala.

Rev the engine, peel off down the street.

Debbie takes it all in.


EXT. STREET - DAY

Debbie, on another street crowded with shops.

Ahead, seated on a bench, three attractive YOUNG LADIES.

And Sean Halsey.  Flirting.

With her phone, Debbie snaps another incriminating picture, then slips past.

A few shops down, she finds her destination.


INT. COMICS SHOP - DAY

The comics shop, crowded with TEENS.

TWO MALE SHOP-OWNERS chat up CUSTOMERS.

In a corner, GAMERS run a role-playing game.

At an aisle, Debbie spots...

...Braydon Wyatt, rifling back issues.

>                    DEBBIE
>           Got any Dick Tracy?

He startles-!

>                    BRAYDON
>           --Ah, shit.  This is my sanctuary,
>           Deb.  Don't fuck with me in my
>           sanctuary.

>                    DEBBIE
>           Who's fuckin' with you?

>                    BRAYDON
>           You don't even like comics.  You
>           want something.

>                    DEBBIE
>           I love comics.

                    BRAYDON
     Then will you do me?  I'm trying to
     get a girl who likes comics to do
     me.

                    DEBBIE
     Someday.

                    BRAYDON
     I'll be dead by someday.

                    BRAYDON (CONT'D)
     At least dress up like Wonder Woman
     and say dirty things to me.

                    DEBBIE
     We'll see.

hakes his head, knows it'll never happen.  Keeps flipping.

                    BRAYDON
     Really, what do you want?

                    DEBBIE
     There's these two guys--

                    BRAYDON
     --I don't like how this is
     startin'.

                    DEBBIE
     The Kirkpatrick brothers.

                    BRAYDON
     ...Yeah...

                    DEBBIE
     You know them?

                    BRAYDON
     Yeah.

                    DEBBIE
     You work with them?

                    BRAYDON
     No.

                    DEBBIE
     They're not, uh, doing anything you
     might know about?

                    BRAYDON
          I can ask around.

                    DEBBIE
          Sure.  That's cool.  But that might
          take a while.  Tell me everything
          you know.  Like, even rumors.

Braydon looks around the shop.

                    BRAYDON
          Buy me some comics.

                    DEBBIE
          I don't have any money.  You're the
          one with the job.

                    BRAYDON
          Broke ass bitch.  All right, what
          else have you got?

                    DEBBIE
          Cigarettes.

                    BRAYDON
          What is this?  Prison?

She's out of ideas.

                    BRAYDON (CONT'D)
          Well at least you're not saying I
          can touch your tits.  I respect you
          for that.
                    (beat)
          Okay.  I'm going to stay here, buy
          six comics like an honest fucking
          citizen, then I will meet you at
          the library.

                    DEBBIE
          The library?  Really?

                    BRAYDON
          No one thinks I go there.  But I
          do.


INT. LIBRARY - DAY

Debbie, at a library table.

Braydon enters, gestures down a row.

ebbie follows.

> DEBBIE
> (whisper)
> Well?

> BRAYDON
> Okay.  Why?

> DEBBIE
> They're causin' trouble for a
> friend.

> BRAYDON
> I heard about that Galbo girl.

> DEBBIE
> Do you know anything?

> BRAYDON
> Not about that.

> DEBBIE
> Okay, the Kirkpatricks.

> BRAYDON
> Small timers.  Vandalism.  A wallet
> or two.  Boosting.  Got banned from
> the comic shop.  They did a tryout
> for my old boss last summer, but
> fucked it up.

> DEBBIE
> Why are small timers digging
> through dumpsters?

> BRAYDON
> ...A pick-up?

> DEBBIE
> You tell me.

e considers.

> BRAYDON
> I heard they move some weed.  Some
> pills.  I'll find out if they're
> into more, but... I think they're
> just losers.

                    DEBBIE
          Oh, they're DEFINITELY losers.
          Ask, but quiet.  And don't mention
          me.

                    BRAYDON
          Yeah, okay.  Oh, Deb -- speaking of
          weed -- you wanna get high?

He pulls out his one-hitter.

                    DEBBIE
          Here?

                    BRAYDON
          It's a perfect place.  Get high,
          read a book.  Mind.  Blown.

                    DEBBIE
          Now I know why you come here.

                    BRAYDON
          Those old ladies at the counter
          never look.  People fucking jack
          off in the computer lab and they
          don't even--

                    DEBBIE
          --Braydon, great, yeah, I don't
          need to know that.
                    (beat)
          Thanks.

                    BRAYDON
          You owe me.

Debbie smiles.  Moves out of the aisle with a wave.

Braydon checks over his shoulder.  Lights the one-hitter,
puffs, coughs.  Keeps it in.


EXT. STOREFRONT CHURCH - DAY

Debbie sits under a tree across the street from the
storefront church.  Just watching.

A car pulls into the alley.  Parks.

Trent Galbo gets out, enters.

Debbie soon follows.

steps to the door.  Locked.

he knocks. No answer.

oes to the service door.  Knocks.  No answer.

XT. SPLIT-LEVEL HOME - DAY

ebbie arrives at Teresa's house.

ings the bell.

> NAT
> (through door)
> Who is it?

> DEBBIE
> It's Debbie.

at opens the door.

> DEBBIE (CONT'D)
> Hi.

> NAT
> Hi.

> DEBBIE
> Can I come in?

NT. SPLIT-LEVEL HOME - LIVING ROOM - DAY - CONTINUOUS

-Debbie enters the house.

he place is bare.  Boxes stacked in the corner.

at falls onto a bean bag in the center of the room.

> NAT
> Dad's not here.

> DEBBIE
> I know.  I saw him at the church,
> but he didn't answer the door when
> I knocked.  I wanted to see if
> there was any news.

at shakes her head, sad.

ebbie looks around.

                    DEBBIE (CONT'D)
          You haven't unpacked.

                    NAT
          I did my stuff.   These boxes are
          Dad's.

                    DEBBIE
          Can I look in them?

                    NAT
          Why?

                    DEBBIE
          I'm a naturally curious person.

                    NAT
          ...I guess.

Debbie opens a box.   Then a second.

                    DEBBIE
          Has your dad always worked for this
          Church of New Life?

                    NAT
          He used to work for Great Things.
          But he switched.

                    DEBBIE
          Great Things?   What happened?

                    NAT
          I think my dad got fired.   They
          treated him bad.

Debbie pulls A FRAMED PICTURE from a box.

Trent, Teresa, Nat, and a WOMAN.

                    DEBBIE
          Is this your mom?

                    NAT
          Yeah.   She left us.

                    DEBBIE
          She's pretty.

She puts the picture back.   Cranes to look closer.

> DEBBIE (CONT'D)
> Do you have more pictures?

Nat gets up from the bean bag, crosses to a box, opens the flaps, and hands Debbie a photo album.

> DEBBIE (CONT'D)
> Wow, an album.  Haven't seen these
> in a while.

> NAT
> My mom taught me scrap-booking.

> DEBBIE
> You made this?  I'm impressed.

Debbie flips pages.  Pictures of churches and congregations. Pictures of Teresa -- happy.  Backyard parties and fishing trips.

> DEBBIE (CONT'D)
> These are super cool.

She flips a page--

--does a double-take.

A photograph of Sean Halsey, in a suit.

Debbie shows it to Nat.

> DEBBIE (CONT'D)
> Who's this?

Nat cranes to see.

> NAT
> He worked for Great Things.  He
> used to come by the house.

> DEBBIE
> Why is he in your scrap-book?

> NAT
> I thought he was cute.

> DEBBIE
> Huh.  Do you remember his name?

Nat shakes her head.

                    DEBBIE (CONT'D)
               (playing along)
          You have good taste.  Can I-- Can I
          have this?  I'll bring it back.

                    NAT
          Why?

                    DEBBIE
          He reminds me of someone.  Oh, and
          can I have a picture of your
          sister?

Nat pulls the photograph of Sean from the album, then flips
a few pages.  Finds one of Teresa.

                    DEBBIE (CONT'D)
          Yeah, I like that one.

Nat gently removes the picture.  Hands both to Debbie.

                    NAT
          Do you want to play kickball with
          me in the yard?

                    DEBBIE
          I'd love to.


EXT. SPLIT-LEVEL HOME - DAY

In the backyard of Teresa's house, Debbie and Nat kick a
ball back and forth.  For the first time, Nat looks happy.


INT. RANCH HOUSE - BEDROOM - NIGHT

Debbie enters her bedroom.  Dark outside.  From her pocket,
she pulls out the pictures.

Sets the one of Teresa on her night-stand.

Takes a textbook from her bookbag, stuffs the one of Sean
Halsey into a page.  Shuts it.


INT. RANCH HOUSE - BEDROOM - DAY

Debbie, in her sloppy bed, asleep.

Alarm SOUNDS.  Debbie hits 'snooze.'

fter a moment, her eyes slowly open.

eads the clock.

uddenly-!

> DEBBIE
> Fuck me!

EAPS out of the bed--

SMASH CUT TO:

XT. HIGH SCHOOL - FIELD - DAY

-Debbie high-tails across the field towards Redmont High.

NT. HIGH SCHOOL - CENTRAL OFFICE - DAY

ebbie enters the central office, sheepish.

rincipal Gale stands in her way.

> GALE
> Walk with me, Miss Harlow.

NT. HIGH SCHOOL - HALLWAY - DAY

rincipal Gale walks with Debbie through the halls of
edmont High.  Classes in progress, voices buried behind
alls.

> GALE
> What can we do, Debbie?  What can
> we do?

> DEBBIE
> Am I that close to messin' it up?

> GALE
> It will be a squeaker.  Do you have
> a good excuse?  I might take a good
> excuse.  Recent events and all.

> DEBBIE
> I'm not involved in that.

                    GALE
          Good.  An ATF agent was here this
          morning.  He asked about friends of
          Teresa Galbo.  I told him I saw you
          two at the dance.

                    DEBBIE
          Look.  I have to take my mind off
          it.  All of it.

                    GALE
          How do you intend to do that?

                    DEBBIE
          Actually, Principal Gale, I have
          been thinking about... field
          hockey.


EXT. HIGH SCHOOL - FIELD - DAY

Debbie, in gym cloths, steps onto the practice field with
the FIELD HOCKEY PLAYERS -- high school girls, all legs and
arms.

Sean Halsey blows his whistle, sends the team out for
drills.

He blocks Debbie.

                    SEAN
          Whoa, hold up, there, hot shot.

                    DEBBIE
          I know the rules.

                    SEAN
          Sit this out a bit.  I don't even
          know where to put you.  You might
          suck.

Debbie puts a hand on her hip.

                    DEBBIE
               (come hither)
          Oh, I definitely suck.

Thrown, he drifts to the field line.

                    SEAN
          Just stay here.  And no smoking!

                    DEBBIE
          I gave that up.  This is the new,
          healthier me.

he practice continues.

 TEEN PLAYER gets clobbered in a spill, lands hard on the
rass.  She stands, limps.

ean blows his whistle.

ebbie watches Sean and the Teen Player assess.

he's sent to the sidelines.

rops beside Debbie on the grass.  Lights a cigarette.

ractice continues.

                    DEBBIE (CONT'D)
          That looked painful.

                    TEEN PLAYER
          I pulled a tendon last season.

                    DEBBIE
          Ouch.

                    TEEN PLAYER
          I've seen you around.  Debbie,
          right?  I like how you dress.

                    DEBBIE
          Thanks.  I own, like, nothing.
          Just a bunch of tee shirts.

                    TEEN PLAYER
          Hey, if you want some extra money,
          Mr. Halsey sometimes has us do
          things.

                    DEBBIE
          Things?

                    TEEN PLAYER
          He's part of some youth program
          over at Willsson Street.

                    DEBBIE
          How many of you do it?

                    TEEN PLAYER
          I've done it twice.  It pays, like,
          $7 an hour.  Sometimes he buys us
          pizza.

                    DEBBIE
          I'll think about it.

Sean calls to Debbie.

                    SEAN
          Harlow!

Debbie stamps out her cigarette.

                    SEAN (CONT'D)
          You're in.  Are you stretched?

                    DEBBIE
          Very.

                    SEAN
          Then get in here.  Mid-fielder.
          Know what that is?

                    DEBBIE
               (aside, to Teen Player)
          No fucking clue.

She stands up anyway, runs onto the field.

When she passes Sean, she gives a big, flirty wink.


INT. RANCH HOUSE - LIVING ROOM - NIGHT

Debbie enters her house, stiff as hell, grass-stained.

In pain, she falls into her dad's La-Z-Boy.  Groans.

Brenda emerges from the kitchen.

                    BRENDA
          It's still daylight!

                    DEBBIE
          I joined the field hockey team.

Brenda laughs.

                    BRENDA
          Well you're full of surprises.

                    DEBBIE
          Water... please... water.

                    BRENDA
          Tylenol?

                    DEBBIE
          Yes.  Drugs.  Yes.

                    BRENDA
          Stop sweating in your daddy's
          chair.

Brenda returns to the kitchen.

Debbie melts onto the carpet.

                    DEBBIE
          Fuck me.


INT. RANCH HOUSE - BEDROOM - NIGHT

Debbie lays on her bed in the dark.

The clock: 11:17 PM.

On her night table -- the picture of Teresa.

She stares at it in the moonlight.

  SWELL to--

                                        SMASH CUT TO:


EXT. RANCH HOUSE - NIGHT

--Debbie drops out of her bedroom window and speeds off into
the night.


EXT. STOREFRONT CHURCH - NIGHT

The Church of New Life -- quiet and dark.

Debbie returns to the service door.

Takes out her screwdrivers.

Hard to open.  In time, it gives.

INT. STOREFRONT CHURCH - SORTING AREA - NIGHT

Debbie enters The Church of New Life's sorting area.

Moon through the transom.

Debbie lights her phone's flashlight.

Cuts around racks of hung and sorted clothes--


INT. STOREFRONT CHURCH - MAIN ROOM - NIGHT - CONTINUOUS

--into the main room.

Dimmers run the floor, outline the altar and aisle.

Debbie picks up a Bible from a stack.  Opens it.  A normal
Bible.  Picks up a second.  Flips pages.  Normal.

A third.  Blank pages.

A fourth.  Blank pages.

Sets the books down with a shrug.

Opens the candle box, digs through the votives, scours the
bottom of the box.

With her phone's flashlight, she detects...

...a hidden latch, underneath.

She opens this secret chamber.

Inside is a bound book -- a ledger.

She only has a few seconds to fan the pages when--

--BANG (O.S.)!

The service door in the other room.  Opens/shuts.

Light strikes the altar from a bulb around the corner.

Debbie drops the ledger back into the chamber.

DUCKS behind the altar.

A shadow hits the door between the rooms.

Hunched shoulders, a person struggles with something.

OUND (O.S): low male voices.

hen--

-the light goes OUT.

he service door opens and shuts once more.

ebbie holds in the dark.

lowly... she comes out of hiding--

NT. STOREFRONT CHURCH - SORTING AREA - NIGHT - CONTINUOUS

-Debbie, without her flashlight, fumbles her way to the orting area.

mpty. As she inspects--

-the service door SWINGS OPEN yet again!

he's face-to-face with...

..the Pudgy Man.

ne of the two that took Teresa.

he man's clearly startled. And before he does anything--

-Debbie KICKS OUT and knocks the wind out of him.

he races into the main room-!

NT. STOREFRONT CHURCH - MAIN ROOM - NIGHT - CONTINUOUS

-The main room.

ebbie tumbles across the altar and--

-SPRAWLS into the first row of plastic chairs.

truggles back up, tangled in chairs.

akes it to the front door just as--

-she's tackled!

agged to the floor -- Pudgy Man on top of her.

                    PUDGY MAN
          What are you doing here!

She can't answer -- his hands grip her throat.

She gets an arm loose, pulls his beard!

The Pudgy Man yelps in pain.

A second man appears in the open doorway.

The Heavy Man -- the second kidnapper.

                    PUDGY MAN (CONT'D)
               (to the Heavy Man)
          What should we do with her?

                    HEAVY MAN
          Is she breathing?

                    PUDGY MAN
          Should I-- Should I-?

                    HEAVY-SET MAN
          Give her one to the head.

CLANG!

A wrench lands on the floor.

Debbie can barely breathe!

The Pudgy Man lets go of her throat, grabs the wrench.

Debbie watches it happen--

--WHAM!

                                        BLACK.


FADE IN ON:


EXT. PARK - NIGHT

Debbie opens her eyes.  Night-time.

She's laying on her back in dewy grass.

Her head bleeds -- jacket and tee covered in spotted red.

She sits up.

A public park.  Alone.

She dabs her wound.  Ouch.

Wobbles to her feet.

Reaches into her jacket.

Her mobile phone is smashed.

Same pocket, a pack of crushed cigarettes.

Lights a broken one.

Does a 360.  Yes.  All alone.


INT. RANCH HOUSE - BATHROOM - NIGHT

In her bathroom, Debbie cleans her head wound.

Blood.  Sticky.  Everywhere.

She braces herself on the sink.

A welt at the hairline.

Wobbling, she undresses.


INT. RANCH HOUSE - BEDROOM - NIGHT

Debbie exits her bathroom in bra and panties.

Struggles to her bed, falls face down.  Out.

                              DISSOLVE TO:

INT. RANCH HOUSE - BEDROOM - DAY

Debbie, same spot on her bed.  Unmoved.  Unconscious.

SOUND: her alarm.  Beep!  Beep!  Beep!

Cole Harlow enters.

Goes to the alarm.  Switches it off.

He touches his daughter's shoulder.

                    COLE
          Debbie.  You over-slept again.
          Come on.  Get up.  Get up!

No response.

                    COLE (CONT'D)
          Debbie.  Deborah Lynn!  You hear
          me?

Shakes her -- harder.

Rolls her over.

Notices: blood on her pillow.

                    COLE (CONT'D)
          Oh, shit!
                (calling out)
          Brenda!  Brenda!


INT. HOSPITAL ROOM - DAY

Debbie.  Pale.  Eyes closed.

Her wound has been dressed.

She's propped in a bed in a private hospital room.

Her eyes flit open.

Beside her in a chair:

A man with an off-putting smile.

                    SURRETT
          Hello, Miss Harlow.  My name is
          Agent Charles Surrett.  Federal
          Bureau of Alcohol, Tobacco, and
          Firearms.  You can call me Chuck.

CHUCK SURRETT -- 30s, brown coat and slicked hair -- looks
younger.  Was a boy who was hoped to, perhaps, grow more
handsome as he aged, but he hasn't.  Behind the eyes -- man
stories.  Most of them bad.

                    SURRETT (CONT'D)
          Nasty bump.

Debbie fingers her bandages.

SURRETT (CONT'D)
But you're a tough pain in the ass.
Those were your father's words.

DEBBIE
(a croak)
Sounds more like my step-mother's.

e grins.

SURRETT
How does a girl go to bed perfect
and wake up -- or should I say NOT
wake up -- with a concussion.
(beat)
Ah, but you're a teenager.
Unpredictable. I have two-- no,
three-- daughters. Is this what I
have to look forward to?
(beat)
What happened?

DEBBIE
I don't remember.

SURRETT
What can you remember?

DEBBIE
Field hockey.

SURRETT
You were at practice from 3:35 to
4:45 yesterday. In fact, you're
missing practice right now.

DEBBIE
Where is Teresa Galbo?

SURRETT
Is that bump connected to your
friend?

DEBBIE
I told you. I can't remember.

SURRETT
The bad guys only hurt the witness
when the witness is involved.
Someone sees something once, it
goes on the record, that's that.
(MORE)

                    SURRETT(CONT'D)
          So why hurt them?  You hurt them
          because there's a connection.

Debbie keeps mum.

                    SURRETT (CONT'D)
          Next time, it might not be just a
          knock on the head.  So, why don't
          you tell me what's really going on?

                    DEBBIE
          I have a headache.

                    SURRETT
          Take some aspirin.

                    DEBBIE
          Are my parents outside?

                    SURRETT
          Yes.

                    DEBBIE
          Get them.

He huffs.  Leans in.

                    SURRETT
          I'm just trying to find your
          friend.
                    (beat)
          Why don't you tell me something
          that helps us both.

                    DEBBIE
          I'll show you mine if you show me
          yours.

                    SURRETT
          Oh, I like you, Debbie Harlow.  I
          really do.

He smiles.

                    SURRETT (CONT'D)
          I'll tell you this because it's
          public record.  The Evanston Sun,
          August 18, three years ago.
                    (beat)
          Now show me yours.

She bites her lip.

                    DEBBIE
          ...There's a guy who pisses on a
          dumpster next to the drug store.
          He might know what's inside that
          dumpster besides the trash.

Surrett reaches out.  Brushes back her hair.  Checks the
welt, the bandage.

Debbie doesn't move.

                    SURRETT
          Nasty bump.

He's gone.

She can breath.


INT. CAR - MOVING - DAY

Cole drives, Debbie rides, Brenda in the back.

Silence until:

                    COLE
          I don't want you sneakin' out
          anymore, baby doll.  We know you're
          older and, and you're gonna do
          whatever the fuck you want--

                    BRENDA
          --Cole--

                    COLE
          --but no sneakin' out.  Promise.

                    DEBBIE
          I can't.  I'm a night person.

                    BRENDA
              (grrr)
          You're gonna end up like your
          friend.

                    COLE
          Just stay out of it.
              (beat)
          You're not breaking the law or--

                    DEBBIE
          --Dad--

                    COLE
          --Just stay out of it.  Please.
          And don't miss any more goddamn
          school.


INT. HIGH SCHOOL - CLASSROOM - DAY

Debbie, in class, barely listens.

Bruise on her head.

CU:
Her notebook.  A list and a diagram.  The facts so far.


EXT. SPLIT-LEVEL HOME - DAY

Debbie, bookbag over shoulder, knocks on the door to the
Galbo house.

Trent Galbo answers, rumpled, hasn't slept a wink.

                    GALBO
          Hello, Debbie.  What happened to
          your-?

Indicates her injury.

                    DEBBIE
          --Oh.  Nothing.  I hit my head on a
          door.  It's actually gone down a
          lot.  Is Nat here?

                    GALBO
          I'll call her-- Nat!  Nat!

                    DEBBIE
          I wanted to see if she could go to
          the playground.

                    GALBO
          That's appreciated.  Thank you.

                    DEBBIE
          Oh, and the library.  Is that okay?

                    GALBO
          Fantastic.  I don't take her nearly
          enough.  She has a card.

at appears in the doorway.

                    GALBO (CONT'D)
          Are you done with your homework?

                    NAT
          Yes.

                    GALBO
          Good.  Debbie wants to take you to
          the park and the library.

                    NAT
          Yay!

                    GALBO
          Grab your library card.  It's in
          the jar. Back by supper.  And don't
          wander off.  Stay with Debbie.

he girl nods, grabs a jacket, and she's out the door.

s Debbie moves away from the house.

n eye back to Galbo, still watching.


XT. PLAYGROUND - DAY

ebbie and Nat cross the playground where they first met.
ind blows, clouds overhead, chillier.

                    DEBBIE
          How's your dad?

                    NAT
          The other night I went to get a
          drink of water and he was crying
          downstairs.

ey enter the playground; CHILDREN jump and run.

ebbie stops.  Sets down her bookbag.

                    DEBBIE
          What if we just play a little, and
          then we go do something, okay?

                    NAT
          What?

                    DEBBIE
          Well.  I need your help.


EXT. STREET - DAY

Nat and Debbie, crouched across the street from the
Kirkpatrick house.

In the driveway, the blue Chevy Impala.

Debbie pulls a notebook from her bookbag, scrawls something
on sheet.  Rips it out, folds it.

                    DEBBIE
          You're small.  This'll be no
          problem.  Just, uh, see that car?
          The blue one?  Put this under the
          windshield wiper on the driver's
          side.  Got it?

                    NAT
          The boys who pushed me have Teresa?

                    DEBBIE
          I don't think so.  But I want to
          talk to them.

                    NAT
          Then why don't you go up and knock?

Debbie cradles Nat's chin.

                    DEBBIE
          I'm not much of a go-up-and-knock
          kinda gal.

She tucks the slip into Nat's hand.

                    DEBBIE (CONT'D)
          Don't let them see you.

Nat slips between some hedges.

Works her way along.

Bends alongside the Impala.  Lifts the windshield wiper.
Places the note.

The screen door of the house BANGS OPEN!

Jason and Kelly Kirkpatrick.

Debbie gasps, prepares to intercede!

Nat dives behind trash cans alongside the garage.

The Kirkpatricks hop in their Impala, rev the engine, and back out of the drive.

Full stop.

Jason, behind the wheel, reaches out of the window.

Snatches the note from the wiper.

Then peels out.

Nat, from the trash cans, gives a thumbs up.

EXT. LIBRARY - DAY

Debbie and Nat climb the steps of the library.

                    DEBBIE
          You're a brave kid.

She tousles the younger girl's hair.

                    NAT
          That was fun!  What's next, what's
          next?

INT. LIBRARY - DAY

Nat, in the library's kid's section.

Debbie steps into the zone.  Taps Nat's shoulder.

                    DEBBIE
          Okay, now let's look for my friend.

                    NAT
          Did you find your article?

                    DEBBIE
          Yep.  They had it in the newspaper
          section.  Memorized it.  Here in my
          noggin.

Moving along, the two comb rows at the library, on a hunt.

                    DEBBIE (CONT'D)
          My friend sometimes comes here.

Debbie slows, sees something.

                    DEBBIE (CONT'D)
          Wait here.  Don't move.

She parts from Nat, sneaks to the shelves.

POV:
Sean Halsey, in a corner, with the Teen Player from the
field hockey team.  Touching her inappropriately.

Debbie takes out her phone.  Snaps a pic on the sly.

Returns to Nat.

                    NAT
          Was that your friend?

                    DEBBIE
          Hell no.  He's a bad egg.

                    NAT
          So where do we look next?

                    DEBBIE
          We could check the computer lab,
          but we'd need in a biohazard suit.

                    NAT
          What's a biohazard suit?

                    DEBBIE
          Never mind.  Let's go.  My friend
          must be somewhere else.


INT. COMICS SHOP - DAY

Debbie and Nat enter the comics shop.

No Braydon Wyatt.

                    DEBBIE
          He's not here either.

She thinks.

                    DEBBIE (CONT'D)
          There's one more place, but I don't
          want you to go there.  I'll walk
          you home, okay?

                    NAT
          But I want to help!

ebbie bends to Nat.

                    DEBBIE
          I know.  I know.  And you did soooo
          good today.  I'll think up other
          ways you can help me, okay?

                    NAT
          Like what?

                    DEBBIE
          Like...

ebbie notices something outside the shop -- a face in the
isplay glass.  Trent Galbo?

                    DEBBIE (CONT'D)
          I think I saw your dad outside.

he steps to the window, scans the sidewalk.

EOPLE, but not Galbo.

                    NAT
          Maybe he's looking for me.  I
          should get home.

                    DEBBIE
          I'll walk you.  But, Nat.  Don't
          tell him what we did today, okay?

                    NAT
          Don't tell Dad?

                    DEBBIE
          Just for now.  I don't want you
          getting into trouble.

T. STREET - DAY

ebbie walks a sparse street.

ut businesses, foreclosed homes.

Comes upon a warehouse, goes around back--


EXT. WAREHOUSE - DAY - CONTINUOUS

--Debbie, at the rear corner of the warehouse, finds a stack
of crates in the shape of a staircase.

Leads up to a cracked window.

She climbs them, peers inside.

POV:
Wide space.  Dirty.  Empty.

SOUND: muffled, echoing voices.

She opens the window, drops a leg over the other side.


INT. WAREHOUSE - DAY

Debbie balances on a stack of lumber set against the other
side of the window.

When she jumps to the ground, she knocks a 4 x 4 off the
stack and it lands with a--

--SMACK!

The muffled voices stop.

Debbie holds.  Makes a face.

From the door to an adjacent room emerges...

...Braydon Wyatt.

                    BRAYDON
          Deb, what the fuck?

                    DEBBIE
          It's okay.  I'm alone.

                    BRAYDON
              (over shoulder)
          It's a friend.

Braydon crosses the space.

Muffled voices resume.

                    DEBBIE
          Who's in there?

                    BRAYDON
          What do you care?  I'm surprised
          you remembered this place.

                    DEBBIE
          I'm surprised you still use it.
          It's fucking cold.

e hitches his thumb to the other room.

                    BRAYDON
          Some girls don't mind the cold.
          Why you lookin' for me?

                    DEBBIE
          I need two things.  And I don't
          have much time.

                    BRAYDON
          Heh.  I bet.  What?

                    DEBBIE
          I need $300 worth of weed by
          tomorrow.

                    BRAYDON
          You serious?

                    DEBBIE
          Don't worry, I'm not gonna sell it.
          It's for a special project.  But it
          can't be, like, some fucking little
          dime bag.  It has to be impressive.
          And it has to be good.

                    BRAYDON
          Do you have $300?

e puts his hand out.

                    DEBBIE
          Not yet.  Can you meet me at the
          library tomorrow after school?

                    BRAYDON
          All right.  What's the second
          thing?

> DEBBIE
> I want you to keep an eye on me.

> BRAYDON
> Why?

> DEBBIE
> Because I think someone might try
> to hurt me.

He looks over his shoulder.

> BRAYDON
> Deb.

> DEBBIE
> Don't bail.  Don't you fucking
> bail.  You work for a big time guy
> and do dangerous shit all the time.

> BRAYDON
> (groans)
> Okay, okay.  I'll watch your ass.
> But, I fucking want something from
> you.

Debbie raises her brow.

> BRAYDON (CONT'D)
> (intense)
> You're gonna dress up like Wonder
> Woman for me.

She laughs.

> DEBBIE
> Jesus, okay.  Sure.  Whatever.

> BRAYDON
> Time and place of my choosing.

> DEBBIE
> Jesus.  Fine.


EXT. PLAYGROUND - DUSK

Jason and Kelly Kirkpatrick, atop the Jungle Gym at the
playground, impatient.  Eyes to the setting sun.

Across the grass, Debbie approaches.

                    KELLY
          Look!

                    JASON
          Oh, fuck.  Not her.

ebbie comes within spitting distance.

hey hop down.

                    DEBBIE
          Hello, my little fuck ups.

                    JASON
          Bitch, I owe you an ass kicking.

                    DEBBIE
          Go ahead.  Pop me in the kisser.

                    JASON
          Can't.  Waitin' on somebody.

                    DEBBIE
          Yeah.  Me!

                    KELLY
          That note was from you?

                    DEBBIE
          I've got a business proposition.
          Peace.

he holds out her hand to shake.

                    JASON
          No.  No, no.  My fucking ribs still
          hurt.  Kickin' a man when he's down
          is mutha-fuckin' bullshit.

                    DEBBIE
          Pushing a 10-year-old is
          mutha-fuckin' bullshit.  So.  Even.

ason, reluctant, takes her hand.  Shakes on it, a bit
eery.  His brother does the same.

                    JASON
          How'd you know that was our car?

                    DEBBIE
          Oh, I know everything.  Like that
          the police are onto your little
          pill pick-up.  That drug store
          shares the same dumpster as the
          church.  I suggest you skip the
          next few drops.  They're watchin'.

                    KELLY
          How you know about that?

                    JASON
          And why warn us?  You fuckin' hate
          us.  Give you a thrill to have us
          get caught.

                    DEBBIE
          Hey, I don't want you caught.  I
          need two bigggg, stroooong boys
          with worldly ambition and bad
          morals.

                    JASON
          This better be worth it.

                    DEBBIE
          $300 bucks in weed.  Good stuff.
          Yours to sell for triple that
          price.

The brothers pass a look.  It's good.

                    DEBBIE (CONT'D)
          Okay.  Great.  First.  I need your
          car.


INT. CAR - MOVING - DUSK

Jason drives the Impala.  Kelly, shotgun.  Debbie, in the
backseat, leaned between the two.

                    JASON
          What time is it?

Debbie looks at her phone.

                    DEBBIE
          Almost nine.

                    JASON
          Is the place still open?

> DEBBIE
> We'll make it.  We need to pick up
> something first from Halloweentown.

> JASON
> Halloweentown?

NT. CAR - NIGHT

he Impala, parked.

ason, Kelly, Debbie, in same positions.

nly now, the boys wear...

..cheap plastic Halloween masks.

> DEBBIE
> I don't know which is uglier --
> those masks or your real faces.

> JASON
> Ha ha.  Where is this fucking guy?
> He better show or I'm ditching.

he checks her phone.

> DEBBIE
> We may have to sit a minute.

EVEAL:

ign: "WILLSSON STREET"

clubhouse on a residential street.

lacard in the window:

YOUTH CENTER"

ddenly!  Lights inside the Youth Center douse and...

..out comes Sean Halsey.

ccompanied by THREE GIRLS, none recognized.

kisses each on the cheek and they all wave goodbye.

ean watches them go, turns.

ason and Kirk duck out of sight.

>           DEBBIE (CONT'D)
>      He can't see us.  We're not under
>      the streetlight.

Slowly, the boys rise again.

>           DEBBIE (CONT'D)
>      Pull around back.


EXT. YOUTH CENTER - NIGHT

Sean makes his way to a parked sports car, keys out.

GRABBED!

Jason and Kelly overpower him--

--tape his mouth shut, bind his hands--

--throw a sack over his head.

TOSS him into the trunk of the car.

Kelly seals the bumper with a wire.

Fast, the brothers are back in the front seat.

SOUND (O.S.): from the trunk -- kicking, muffled yelling.

Jason, winded.

>           JASON
>      Told ya we knew how to do that.

>           DEBBIE
>      I shudder to think how you
>      practiced.

>           KELLY
>      Don't worry -- no one's ever been
>      in that trunk that didn't deserve
>      to be.

>           JASON
>      Who is this guy?

>           DEBBIE
>      He's a teacher at my school.

>           JASON
>      Oh shit.

                    DEBBIE
          And he TOTALLY deserves it.

XT. FIELD - NIGHT

he Chevy Impala.  In a field.  Way out of town.

tars above, night sounds.

o one for miles.  Except.

ebbie.  Jason.  Kelly.

n an arc around the closed trunk.

                    DEBBIE
          Open it.

                    JASON
          He'll see your face.

                    DEBBIE
          Open it.

ason huffs.

                    JASON
          You're one crazy bitch.

ason and Kelly set their Halloween masks.

elly unwinds the wire and springs open the trunk.

nside, Sean squirms like a caught fish.

ason takes off the sack.

veaty, wide-eyed, Sean recognizes Debbie.

ebbie RIPS the tape off his mouth; Sean SCREAMS!

                    DEBBIE
          Hey there, Mr. Halsey.

                    SEAN
          What the FUCK, Debbie!  Jesus
          Christ!

e writhes against his bindings.

                    DEBBIE
          Better not yell at me, Mr. Halsey.
          I've had a bad blow to the head.
          It's messin' with my judgment.

Debbie takes out her phone.

                    DEBBIE (CONT'D)
          You're gonna wanna see these.

She flips through the pictures of Sean with the younger
girls.

                    DEBBIE (CONT'D)
          I've got dozens more.  A lot worse
          ones.  I bet Principal Gale would
          love to see these.  Maybe the
          police.
                    (to Jason and Kelly)
          Boys, take a hike.  I'd like some
          alone time.

The Kirkpatricks wander into the field.

                    SEAN
          You think anyone cares that I screw
          some 17-year-olds?  They NEVER
          care.

                    DEBBIE
          I know some people that care about
          what happened at Great Things.

                    SEAN
          W-- What do you know about Great
          Things?

Debbie slips a pack of cigarettes from her jacket.  Lights
one.  Puffs.

                    DEBBIE
          Read about it at the lie-berry.
          Missing cash.  Missing pastor's
          wife.  Drug trafficking.  Sex
          trafficking.  All that jazz.
          Evanston Sun has a helluva junior
          reporter on their staff.

                    SEAN
          Not anymore.  Someone saw to that.
          But it wasn't me.  Let me go.

omes in close.

>                    DEBBIE
>          Awww.  Don't worry, Mr. Halsey.  I
>          don't believe everything I read.

he squeezes his cheeks.

ean snaps.

>                     SEAN
>          You and your FUCK BUDDIES back
>          there are small time!  You're way
>          over your skis.  You're just a high
>          school cunt.

>                    DEBBIE
>          I'll tell you how small time we
>          are.  I paid these guys with $300
>          worth of marijuana.  For that,
>          they're willing to murder you.
>          Because when you're small time...
>          nothing fucking matters.

ean, at last, registers fear.

>                 DEBBIE (CONT'D)
>          Where's Teresa Galbo?

>                     SEAN
>          I don't know where they took her.
>          She's been traded around since
>          Sunday.  She's too hot right now.
>          Yesterday, they were gonna kill
>          her.

>                    DEBBIE
>          Who was?

>                     SEAN
>          Can't tell you that.

ebbie snaps her fingers.

ason and Kelly, in masks, come forward.

ason takes Sean's arms, pulls them over the trunk latch.
elly reaches to slam the trunk hatch, break his arms.

>                 SEAN (CONT'D)
>          No!  No!  Don't!

                    DEBBIE
          I need you to create some options,
          Mr. Halsey.

                    SEAN
          All right.  All right!  Stop.
               (beat)
          Tomorrow.  I can get you an address
          during school tomorrow.  They move
          her every day, but I can... I think
          I can get you an address.

Debbie signals.  Kelly reaches again for the trunk hatch.

                    SEAN (CONT'D)
          No!  I'll do it!  I swear.  I'll
          get you the address by, by noon
          tomorrow.  Teresa will be there for
          24 hours.

                    DEBBIE
          What if they kill her first?

                    SEAN
          It's all I can do.

Debbie tucks Sean's arms back inside the trunk.

Kelly slams it shut.


EXT. COUNTRY ROAD - NIGHT

The Impala ZOOMS on a country road.

Stops on an isolated stretch.

Jason and Kelly get out, wrestle Sean from the trunk.

Take off his bindings.

The Impala speeds away in the dark.

Sean starts walking.


INT. CAR - MOVING - NIGHT

The Impala.  Debbie and the Kirkpatricks hit the main drag.

Debbie touches her head injury.

or a moment, looks exhausted, perhaps overwhelmed.

>                    JASON
>           So where's the smoke?  It's nearly
>           one in the morning and I'm tired.

>                    DEBBIE
>           I'll have it by four o'clock
>           tomorrow afternoon.

ason slams on the brakes.

>                    JASON
>           Fuck!  You don't have the stuff ON
>           YOU?

>                    DEBBIE
>           I never said I did.  I just said
>           I'd get it for you.  My guy is
>           bringing it to me tomorrow.

ason shakes his head, looks to his brother.

>                    JASON
>           We need to be better negotiators...
>                    (intense)
>           Debbie Fucking Harlow.  If you
>           don't have our weed by four, we
>           can't be responsible for what we
>           might do to you.

ebbie gives them both kisses on the cheeks.

>                    DEBBIE
>           Sealed with a kiss.  I owe you.
>           For more than you think.  If you
>           hadn't shoved Nat Galbo on the
>           playground, I wouldn't have met her
>           sister.  So... thank you, boys!

ason wipes the kiss from his cheek.

ebbie opens the car door.

>                    DEBBIE (CONT'D)
>           I can walk it from here.  The
>           playground.  Four o'clock tomorrow.
>           See ya laters, alligators!

ey watch her go.  Jason puts the car into 'drive.'

                    JASON
          That fucking girl.  What a
          nightmare.

                    KELLY
          I kinda like her.

                    JASON
          Yeah...  I kinda like her, too.

The Impala peels away, into the night.


INT. RANCH HOUSE - BEDROOM - NIGHT

Debbie climbs through her bedroom window.

Pitch black.

Light snaps on!

Brenda sits upright on Debbie's bed.

Debbie, shamed, but only briefly.

                    BRENDA
          Your poor father.

                    DEBBIE
          Where is he?

                    BRENDA
          Sleeping.  He has to work early.

Debbie kicks off her shoes, starts to change.

                    BRENDA (CONT'D)
          I'll tell him you're okay.
                    (beat)
          Are you okay?  Debbie?

                    DEBBIE
          I'm going through something right
          now, but it's over tomorrow.

                    BRENDA
          We can help.  We want to help.

Debbie sits on the bed.  Hugs a stuffed toy.

                    DEBBIE
          Thanks.  I'll be all right.

                    BRENDA
          How do you know that whatever this
          is will be over by tomorrow?

                    DEBBIE
          ...Because it has to be.


INT. HIGH SCHOOL - HALLWAY - DAY

Debbie, between classes, in the locker bay.

Down the hall, coming her way, Sean Halsey, a wreck.
Limping.  Pale.  Exhausted.

When they cross paths, he hands her...

..a piece of paper.

                    SEAN
          Miss Harlow.  I trust I'll see you
          after school?  Five o'clock.  No
          later.

She opens the note:

Hardy slip with an address written in the body:

"1927 SHAW STREET"

                    DEBBIE
          What about field hockey, Mr.
          Halsey?

                    SEAN
               (bitter)
          Practice is canceled.

He's off down the hall.


INT. HIGH SCHOOL - LUNCHROOM - DAY

Debbie, in line at the school lunchroom.  Stands with empty
tray.  When the line moves, she BREAKS for a side door--


EXT. HIGH SCHOOL - DAY - CONTINUOUS

--Debbie slips out, sets her tray on top of a hedge, and
flees the campus.

INT. SIM'S GARAGE - DAY

Debbie arrives at Sim's Garage.

Enters as before, looks for her father.  Finds him under the
hood of a car in the stalls.  Taps his shoulder.

> COLE
> Baby doll -- why aren't you at
> school?

> DEBBIE
> I have a half-day.  Don't you
> remember?

> COLE
> Oh.

> DEBBIE
> And I'm the one with the
> concussion.

> COLE
> Have you eaten?

> DEBBIE
> No.

> COLE
> Let me finish up.  Wait in the
> office.  I'll be there as soon as I
> finish this transmission.

INT. SIM'S GARAGE - OFFICE - DAY

The second Debbie is in the garage office--

--she cracks her compact.  Works the screwdrivers on the
cash register.  SPRINGS open with the soft ding of a bell.

Quick -- she grabs a wad of cash.

> DEBBIE
> Shit.

Not enough.

Pockets the money, looks around.  Digs under the counter.

Finds another CASH BOX.

ets it on the counter.  Works the lock until it breaks.

akes the money -- all of it.

tuffs the cash and her compact into her jacket pockets.

he looks to her right.

ole has been watching her.

                    COLE
          What are you doin', baby doll?
               (beat)
          Did you just steal that money?

ebbie moves around the counter.

                    DEBBIE
          I need it, Dad.

                    COLE
          For what?

                    DEBBIE
          It's important.

                    COLE
          For what, Debbie?

                    DEBBIE
          I can't explain right now.

                    COLE
          Try.

he comes forward and kisses him.

                    DEBBIE
          I have to go--

e grabs her wrist.

                    DEBBIE (CONT'D)
          --Daddy!  I'm sorry.  I'll bring it
          back.  I swear.  You have to trust
          me.  Dad.  You have to trust me.

                    COLE
          Is this the concussion-?

                    DEBBIE
          --No!  It's not my head.  Can't you
          trust me?

                    COLE
          Have you earned that?

                    DEBBIE
          I'm a good person, Daddy.  I'm a
          good person.  I need this money and
          I have to do something really
          fucking important.

She shakes her arm and he releases her.

Eyes meet.

She runs out.


INT. LIBRARY - DAY

Braydon at the stacks in the library.

He pulls a book about criminal justice from the shelf.

Reads a page.

Debbie, breathless, rounds the row.

                    BRAYDON
          I was beginning to think you were
          gonna dust me.

                    DEBBIE
          Sorry.  I'm having a busy day.  Do
          you have it?

From his bookbag, he flashes her the tight bag of weed.

She hands him the money, stuffs the package in her jacket.

                    DEBBIE (CONT'D)
          Remember our deal.

                    BRAYDON
          Watch you.  I know.  Where you
          gonna be?

She looks at her phone.

                    DEBBIE
          I have to go to the park, then I'm
          going here.

hows him the tardy slip with the address.

                    BRAYDON
          Okay.  I'll watch you.

                    DEBBIE
          But not close.  Stay, uh, kinda out
          of the way, okay?

e nods.

                    DEBBIE (CONT'D)
          Shit.  Gotta go.  Gonna be late.
          Thanks.

he leaves.

e puts back the book.


XT. PLAYGROUND - DAY

ason and Kelly stand next to the parked Impala.

moke cigarettes, kill time.

he playground.  Empty.

                    JASON
          I knew that bitch would be late.

                    KELLY
                (checks)
          It's only five minutes.

                    JASON
          It's just rude, you know?  Come on,
          let's walk over.

ANG!  Loud GUNSHOT!

ason -- struck by a bullet to the head.

rumples to the pavement.

elly ducks down!

he GUNMAN points through the open car window, takes aim.

                         KELLY
          No, don't, don't!

BANG!  He collapses beside his brother.

The Gunman circles the car.

Finds Kelly crawling away, bleeding.

BANG!  A third shot finishes him.

REVEAL:

The gunman.  Sean Halsey.

Sean tosses the weapon into the car.

Removes a pair of gloves, stuffs them in his pocket.

Checks around.  No one saw.

Leaves the scene.


EXT. PLAYGROUND - DAY

Debbie crosses towards the playground.

Checks the time: 4:11 PM.

                         DEBBIE
            Shit.

Arrives at the Jungle Gym.

No Kirkpatricks.

Scans, spots--

--the Chevy Impala, in the adjacent parking lot.

Walks towards it.

Slows when she notices...

...two lumps next to the driver's side door.

Jason.  Kelly.  Dead.

She scans the horizon.  Then peers inside the car.

Keys in the ignition.  Gun on the passenger floor mat.

eyes back to the bloody bodies.

She is confused, terrified.  But decides.

Debbie hops into the Impala!  Peels out.


EXT. CAR - MOVING - DAY

The Impala -- moving fast.  Debbie's speeding again.

She lifts the gun from the floor, checks for bullets.

Tucks the gun in her jacket, next to the weed.


EXT. STREET - DAY

The Impala turns onto an overgrown side street, draped in trees.

Debbie parks.  Hops out.

Starts walking--


EXT. NEIGHBORHOOD - DAY - CONTINUOUS

--Debbie makes a line through a neighborhood, uses backyards to cut to the next block.

Walks a few more houses.  Counts numbers.

There it is.  A run-down Victorian.

1927 Shaw Street.


EXT. VICTORIAN HOME - DAY - CONTINUOUS

Debbie stands at the front door.

Cautious, she peeks into windows.  Can't see a thing.

Knocks.  Knocks again.

At last, the door squeaks open.

There stands...

...Braydon Wyatt.

A deeply sad look on his face.

Flustered, Debbie begins to speak, but--

> BRAYDON
> --Shut up.  Don't say anything.

He gestures.

In his hand, a pistol.

She follows his direction inside.


INT. VICTORIAN HOME - DAY - CONTINUOUS

Braydon slams the door.  Bolts it.

The home is practically empty.

A mattress with fitted sheet is set on the floor.

Table lamp beside.

Emerging from the kitchen...

> SEAN (O.S.)
> Debbie Harlow.

...Sean Halsey.

Debbie calmly glances around a corner, then up the stairs to
the second floor.  No one else home.  No other easy exits.

Just Braydon and Sean box her in.

> SEAN (CONT'D)
> I really didn't think you'd come
> alone.  Pretty stupid.  I brought
> my right-hand man.  You know this
> cat?

Debbie betrays nothing.

> SEAN (CONT'D)
> I love this guy.  B-boy -- you know
> this funky lady?

> BRAYDON
> Nope.  She go to Redmont?

                    SEAN
          A junior.  You like older girls,
          don't you?  Their tits are bigger.

Sean steps forward.

                    SEAN (CONT'D)
          I'm gonna search you.

He begins to pat her down.

                    SEAN (CONT'D)
          Don't worry.  I'll keep my bargain.
          But I need something from you
          first.

Sean easily finds the gun.

                    SEAN (CONT'D)
          This looks familiar.

He digs a couple fresh bullets from his pocket.  Reloads.

                    SEAN (CONT'D)
          Guess I'll have to dump it in the
          river when we're done.  Pretty dumb
          of you and your amateur friends not
          to cover your license plate last
          night.

He pats-down Debbie's chest, almost fondles her.

Finds the bag of marijuana.

                    SEAN (CONT'D)
          Whoa.  Didn't expect this from you,
          Debs.  Major habit.  Here, you keep
          this, I got a truck-full.

He taps the bundle back into her jacket.

                    SEAN (CONT'D)
          I have to admit -- what you did to
          me last night kind of turned me on.

                    DEBBIE
          Where's Teresa?

                    SEAN
          She was here yesterday.  But now
          she's somewhere else.  I know the
                    (MORE)

                    SEAN(CONT'D)
          place.  Braydon and I will take you
          there by six o'clock.  But first...
          I wanted a little alone time.

Sean indicates the mattress.

                    DEBBIE
          Wait a minute--

Debbie, nerves hitting.

                    DEBBIE (CONT'D)
          --I'm not going to fuck you.

Sean tucks the gun in his pants pocket.

Slides onto the mattress.

                    SEAN
          What do you care?  The way you
          flirted with me at school... at
          practice.  I know you want to fuck
          me.  Small price for your friend.

Debbie eyes Braydon.  No reaction.

                    SEAN (CONT'D)
          So... you let me fuck you and I
          become your biggest champion.  Make
          sure you survive the night.
          Believe me, when you meet the guy
          who has Teresa, you're gonna need a
          friend.

                    DEBBIE
          What's his name?

                    SEAN
          His name's Phil.

Debbie -- eyes to Braydon, who nods.

                    BRAYDON
          His name's Phil.

Debbie slowly takes off her jacket.

                    SEAN
          Come.  Sit.

Debbie joins Sean on the mattress.  Lays down stiff.

Braydon does nothing.

> SEAN (CONT'D)
> You can watch, B-boy.  I know you
> want to.

Sean scoots up to Debbie.  Ogles her body.

> SEAN (CONT'D)
> Wow.  Just wow.  You've got
> somethin', Debbie Harlow.

He touches her.  Kisses her neck.

She does nothing.

> SEAN (CONT'D)
> Put some heat into it, will ya?

She opens her mouth.  Touches tongues.

Sean removes her tee shirt, exposes her bra.

> DEBBIE
> (a whisper)
> After this, if you don't take me to
> Teresa, I'm going to kill you.

> SEAN
> Yeah, you do that.

He yanks off her jeans.

She slides back on the mattress, shuts her eyes.

> DEBBIE
> Go easy.  I'm a virgin.

> SEAN
> Ha.  Yeah.  Right.

A look.  Lying?

> SEAN (CONT'D)
> You're not going to bleed on my
> mattress, are you?

She shrugs.

> SEAN (CONT'D)
> Well.  Well, well.  Okay then.  I
> do love new territory...

He unbuckles his belt, starts to move in--

--SMASH!

The table lamp connects with Sean's head!

Sean rolls sideways.

Braydon brings the lamp down again -- HARD.

Sean's out cold.

Braydon reaches into Sean's loose pants, grabs the gun.

Debbie -- stunned.

> BRAYDON
> Sorry.  I had to wait until he was
> distracted.  He's a pretty quick
> draw and I didn't want to take a
> chance.  Whew.  Shit.
> > (beat)
> Are you really a virgin?

> DEBBIE
> Wouldn't you like to know.

She stands up.

> DEBBIE (CONT'D)
> This the prick you work for?  The
> big timer?

> BRAYDON
> Fuck no.  This guy's a total bag of
> dicks.  When you're ready, we'll go
> find your friend.

> DEBBIE
> You know where she is?

> BRAYDON
> Yes.  He told me.

Braydon takes Sean's gun, puts on the safety.

> BRAYDON (CONT'D)
> That's the safety.  You'll have to
> switch it before it'll fire.  Here,
> turn around.

Braydon undoes her bra.

                    DEBBIE
          Um, whatcha doin'?

                    BRAYDON
          Trick I know.

He twists her bra strap, sticks the strap through the
trigger guard, re-snaps the bra.  Then helps Debbie put on
her shirt and jacket.  Taps her back.

                    BRAYDON (CONT'D)
          Yeah.  That works.  His gun is
          small.  Like his cock.  I don't
          think they'll notice it.  Keep your
          back to them.

                    DEBBIE
          To who?

                    BRAYDON
          The bad guys.  Are you ready?

                    DEBBIE
          Yes.  What about him?

Sean, on the floor.

Braydon reaches down, pilfers Sean's pockets, finds keys.

                    BRAYDON
          We'll take his car.

He takes off the fitted sheet from the mattress.  Ties up
Sean.  Takes Sean's shoes.  Drops them out of a window of
the house.

                    BRAYDON (CONT'D)
          He won't catch up to us in time.
          We'll be there and gone.  Back in
          time for homework.

EXT. COUNTRY ROAD - DUSK

Sun goes down over a country road.

INT. CAR - MOVING - DUSK

Braydon drives the country road, Debbie in the passenger
seat of Sean's sports car.

                         DEBBIE
             Do you have a license?

Braydon smiles, shakes his head 'no.'

The car winds past fences onto a dusty road, past bails of
hay and autumn harvest.

Braydon brings the car to a stop in front of...

...a colonial farmhouse.

In the drive, three other cars.

                         DEBBIE (CONT'D)
             Here?

                         BRAYDON
             Yep.

                         DEBBIE
             And his name is Phil?

                         BRAYDON
             Uh huh.  Phil.  He may not look it,
             but he's super fucking ruthless.
             So be careful.

With dread, they step out of the car...

...and move towards the farmhouse's porch.

Braydon draws out his gun, holds it above his head, in
surrender.

He knocks.

A chain is removed.

And the wood door opens.

A THIN MAN -- 50s, gives a nod.

                         THIN MAN
             What do you want, Mr. Wyatt?  And
             who is she?

                         BRAYDON
             She's a customer.  Got a complaint.

                         THIN MAN
             Phil doesn't like complainers.

                    BRAYDON
          Well, I guess it's more of a
          suggestion.

The Thin Man takes Braydon's gun, sets it on a table next to
the door.  Gives a pat-down of Debbie.

                    THIN MAN
          She carrying?

                    BRAYDON
          No.  I checked her.

                    THIN MAN
          Yeah, okay.  They're just finishing
          up.

The Thin Man escorts them inside.


INT. FARMHOUSE - MAIN ROOM - DUSK - CONTINUOUS

Debbie and Braydon are led into the main living space of the
farmhouse.  Big center area with wide windows.

Three archways:

One to the kitchen; one to the bedrooms; one to the exit.

Debbie spots the Heavy Man and the Pudgy Man -- one at each
end of the room.

Upon seeing Debbie, they lean into each other's ears.

Debbie tries to stay cool.

Seated in high-backed chairs in a circle:

An OLD WOMAN -- 70s, almost a wax statue.

A VERY FAT MAN -- 60s, wearing a Fedora hat and a white
suit.

And... to Debbie's great surprise...

Chuck Surrett.

Debbie and Chuck meet eyes.  She's unable to read his face.

The group finishes their chatter.

                    SURRETT
          ...then it's settled.  We'll finish
          off our asset in the bedroom
          tonight.  And then use our friends
          at the firehouse for that little
          problem on MacSwain.

Debbie whispers into Braydon.

                    DEBBIE
               (re: Surrett)
          Is that him?

                    BRAYDON
          The fat one.

This is overheard.

                    VERY FAT MAN
          Can we help you, Mr. Wyatt?

                    BRAYDON
          Sorry, Phil.  No, go ahead and
          finish.

                    VERY FAT MAN
          Where is Mr. Halsey?

                    BRAYDON
          He loaned us his car and sends his
          hellos.  He had business at the
          Youth Center.

                    VERY FAT MAN
          I told you to stick to that slime.
               (to the others)
          Look at this, this baby.  He's one
          of my best, though, even when he
          doesn't quite follow my orders.
          You know, he stole for me a
          beautiful Cadillac.  And he isn't
          even old enough to drive.  It helps
          to start young in this business.
          Say hello, everyone, to the future.

The others say hello, in spooky unison.

                    VERY FAT MAN (CONT'D)
          What do you want, Mr. Wyatt?  Let's
          get you on your way.

                    BRAYDON
          This girl is one of my customers.

                    VERY FAT MAN
          And?

Debbie draws out the package of marijuana.

                    BRAYDON
          I sold her this today.  She wanted
          good stuff, so I got her some.
          Only it's... it's not good.  Burns
          up real funny.

                    VERY FAT MAN
              (to others)
          I don't really care about the
          marijuana trade.  Not much margin
          and it'll probably be legal soon.
          But it's a great litmus test for
          the quality of my suppliers for
          other goods.

The Heavy Man leans into the Very Fat Man, whispers
something.

When finished, the Very Fat Man gives Braydon a look.

                    VERY FAT MAN (CONT'D)
          Mr. Wyatt, is your customer
          affiliated with any other
          organization?

                    BRAYDON
          No, sir.  She just runs some stuff
          through the high school.

                    VERY FAT MAN
          Why was she in The Church of New
          Life on Tuesday night?

The Heavy Man whispers again in the bosses ear.

                    VERY FAT MAN (CONT'D)
              (to Debbie)
          Do you remember anything about
          Tuesday night?

Debbie steps forward.

                    DEBBIE
          Only that I ended up in the
          hospital with a concussion.

                    VERY FAT MAN
          But why.  Why that church?

                    DEBBIE
          I was told there was money for
          stealin'.  These men took the
          pastor's daughter.  I saw them do
          it.  But I told the cops nothing.
          I just had my eyes on that place.
          It was by accident that they found
          me.

The Very Fat Man wags a finger towards Debbie.

The Pudgy Man takes the package from Debbie.  Digs in.
Smells.

                    PUDGY MAN
          Seems okay.

                    VERY FAT MAN
               (to Debbie)
          There are papers on the kitchen
          counter.  Go roll a joint.  We'll
          see how it burns.  If it's all
          good, you're in big trouble for
          wasting my time with such a little
          problem, Mr. Wyatt.

Braydon and Debbie move out of the room--


INT. FARMHOUSE - KITCHEN - DUSK - CONTINUOUS

--to the kitchen.  Country archway back to the bedrooms.

SOUND (O.S.): Conversation continues in the main room.

Debbie dumps out a bud from the bag.

Braydon reaches up her back, unsnaps her bra, hands her
Sean's gun.  She takes off the safety.

Braydon rolls a joint.  Points Debbie down the hall.

                    BRAYDON
               (soft)
          Second door.

Debbie tip-toes down the hall, finds the second door.

Opens it.


INT. FARMHOUSE - BEDROOM - DUSK - CONTINUOUS

Debbie scans the barely-lit bedroom.

Night table, credenza, bed.

No Teresa.

SOUND (O.S.): voices from the main room.

In the corner: a mirror.

In the reflection, Debbie spots--

--hands, bound by rope.

She enters the room.

Teresa!  Gagged in the room's closet.

The two girls meet eyes.

Teresa's widen with surprise.


INT. FARMHOUSE - MAIN ROOM - DUSK

The Very Fat Man is in agreement with Surrett.

                    VERY FAT MAN
          So.  If Galbo won't comply, his
          oldest daughter is of no use to us.
          Kill her first, then we'll next
          take his youngest.  Then, perhaps,
          he'll finally return our missing
          ledger.


INT. FARMHOUSE - BEDROOM - DUSK

Debbie unties Teresa.

                    TERESA
               (hoarse)
          Debbie!  H- how did you get here?

> DEBBIE
> I'll tell you later.

Teresa's hands drop.  Sore, she flexes.

> DEBBIE (CONT'D)
> There's a car outside.

> TERESA
> We can't leave!  They check on me
> every few minutes.

> DEBBIE
> Don't worry -- I have a plan.  You
> go out the window, get in the car,
> I'll go out the front.

> TERESA
> The front!

INT. FARMHOUSE - KITCHEN - DUSK - CONTINUOUS

Braydon has the joint ready.

INT. FARMHOUSE - MAIN ROOM - DUSK - CONTINUOUS

The Very Fat Man calls out from the main room.

> VERY FAT MAN
> What's taking so long to roll that
> joint, Mr. Wyatt!

INT. FARMHOUSE - KITCHEN - DUSK - CONTINUOUS

Braydon looks down the hallway for Debbie.  No sign.

> BRAYDON
> Sorry, Phil -- been a while since I
> rolled one.  I'm used to my
> one-hitter.

> VERY FAT MAN (O.S.)
> Why didn't you say you had a
> one-hitter?  Just use that.

INT. FARMHOUSE - MAIN ROOM - DUSK - CONTINUOUS

The circle is getting restless.

Chuck Surrett, adding things up, starts to sweat.

> VERY FAT MAN
> (to Pudgy Man)
> Go see what's happening.

INT. FARMHOUSE - BEDROOM - DUSK - CONTINUOUS

Debbie tries to open the bedroom window.  Won't budge.

> TERESA
> I think it's nailed.

> DEBBIE
> This works so well at home!

INT. FARMHOUSE - KITCHEN - DUSK - CONTINUOUS

Braydon turns away from the hall and runs into the Pudgy
Man.

> THUG
> Where's that girl?

> BRAYDON
> She went to piss.

The Pudgy Man pushes past--

--Braydon panics.

INT. FARMHOUSE - BEDROOM - DUSK - CONTINUOUS

Debbie and Teresa struggle with the bedroom window.

> BRAYDON (O.S.)
> Debbie!

INT. FARMHOUSE - KITCHEN - DUSK - CONTINUOUS

Braydon jumps on the Pudgy Man, tackles him.

INT. FARMHOUSE - BEDROOM - DUSK - CONTINUOUS

Debbie SHOOTS--

--CRACK!  The window shatters, glass rains down.

INT. FARMHOUSE - MAIN ROOM - DUSK - CONTINUOUS

The Very Fat Man, up from his chair.

Points to the second archway, to the bedrooms.

The Heavy Man takes out a gun.

RUNS towards the bedroom.


INT. FARMHOUSE - BEDROOM - DUSK - CONTINUOUS

Debbie clears glass from the ledge with the barrel.

                    DEBBIE
          Go!

Teresa jumps!

Rolls onto the tall grass beneath the window.


INT. FARMHOUSE - KITCHEN - DUSK - CONTINUOUS

Braydon takes a punch.

The Pudgy Man has the upper hand.


EXT. FARMHOUSE - DUSK - CONTINUOUS

Teresa RUNS from the farmhouse.

Halts, turns.

                    TERESA
          Debbie!


INT. FARMHOUSE - BEDROOM - DUSK - CONTINUOUS

The Heavy Man BURSTS into the bedroom.

Debbie FIRES the gun!

A bullet STRIKES the door, SPLINTERS the wood.

The Heavy Man drops back into the hall.

NT. FARMHOUSE - MAIN ROOM - DUSK - CONTINUOUS

huck Surrett stands!

NT. FARMHOUSE - BEDROOM - DUSK - CONTINUOUS

he Heavy Man FIRES BLINDLY into the bedroom.

ullets SHATTER the lamp, just as--

-Debbie drops out of the window, hard--

XT. FARMHOUSE - NIGHT - CONTINUOUS

-Teresa races for Debbie--

NT. FARMHOUSE - MAIN ROOM - NIGHT - CONTINUOUS

-Surrett, shouting--

> SURRETT
> --Listen!  Listen everybody!  Stop
> and listen-!

NT. FARMHOUSE - KITCHEN - NIGHT - CONTINUOUS

raydon, nose bleeding, on the floor.

he Pudgy Man has grabbed him by the shirt, but holds.

NT. FARMHOUSE - MAIN ROOM - NIGHT - CONTINUOUS

urrett, in the main room.

OUND (O.S.): sirens.

rom under his shirt, Surrett pulls out--

-a badge.

> SURRETT
> Agent Chuck Surrett, ATF!  Stop
> everything you're doing and lay
> down your weapons.  You're under
> arrest.

he Very Fat Man looks confused, then angry.

                         VERY FAT MAN
              I have an excellent lawyer!

                         SURRETT
              We'll see about that, Phil.


EXT. FARMHOUSE - NIGHT - CONTINUOUS

Teresa holds Debbie tight under the bedroom window.

POV:
A half-dozen squad cars--

--a SWAT truck--

--surround the house.

COPS storm the premises.

Teresa and Debbie -- an awkward moment of relief.

Then...

A kiss, melting to smiles.

                                        DISSOLVE TO:


INT. POLICE STATION - OFFICE - DAY

Debbie, in the same police station office as the day after
the kidnapping.  Circled again by Detectives and Uniformed
Officers.  She answers questions.

                                        DISSOLVE TO:


INT. POLICE STATION - OFFICE - DAY

Debbie, in the same office, now alone.

The door opens.

Surrett enters, sits.

                         SURRETT
              Hello again.
                    (beat)
              If I had known you'd keep playing
              detective, I wouldn't have told you
                         (MORE)

                    SURRETT(CONT'D)
          to look up that article.  I did
          that to scare you.  Obviously, it
          didn't work.

                    DEBBIE
          ...I got two guys killed.  Jason
          and Kelly Kirkpatrick.

                    SURRETT
          Sad to say, but that would have
          happened eventually.  And, you're
          the reason, Debbie, that Teresa
          Galbo is still alive, and those one
          of the biggest drug and gun rings
          in the Midwest is behind bars.  You
          and Braydon.

                    DEBBIE
          He said he was working for a big
          timer.  He meant you.

                    SURRETT
          He's going to have a great career
          as an undercover officer, don't you
          think?

XT. POLICE STATION - DAY

ebbie exits the police station.  Clothes and hair a mess.

unlight blinds her eyes.

own the steps of the station, she spots...

..Cole and Brenda.

 few yards away -- Teresa.

ebbie crosses to her parents.

                    DEBBIE
          I want to walk home.

                    COLE
          The police told us everything.  And
          it scares the shit out of us.

                    DEBBIE
          Don't worry, Dad.  This is once in
          a lifetime.

                    COLE
        See you at home, baby doll.  Soon,
        okay?

                    DEBBIE
        Okay.

Kisses on cheeks.  Her parents depart.

Debbie holds a moment, stares at Teresa, who stares back.

Finally, they meet in the middle of the plaza.

                    DEBBIE (CONT'D)
        I'm glad you're not dead.  That
        would have been a terrible
        vacation.

                    TERESA
              (smiles)
        "She's just on vacation."  I
        remember.  But now I'm back!
        Because of you.

Debbie kisses Teresa.

                    TERESA (CONT'D)
        Fucked-up trouble.

                    DEBBIE
        That's me.

The girls walk off, hand in hand.

                                    FADE TO BLACK.


FADE IN ON:


INT. BEDROOM - DAY

Braydon -- in a bedroom filled with comics paraphernalia.

In front of him:

Debbie -- dressed in Wonder Woman costume.  She swings her
hips, blows kisses, caresses her body.  Moans softly,
sexually.

REVEAL:

Teresa, trying not to laugh.

                    TERESA
          Oh my fucking God that's hot.

                    BRAYDON
               (joking)
          Why are you even here?   Seriously.
          Why are you even here?

Debbie cracks up.

                                        BLACKOUT.

                                        THE END.

OTHER SCREENPLAYS IN THIS COLLECTION

OTHER SCREENPLAYS IN THIS COLLECTION

## ABOUT THE AUTHOR

Darren Callahan is an award-winning writer, director, and composer who has written drama for the BBC, SyFy Channel, National Public Radio, and Radio Pacifica New York. His work for theatre has been both commercially and critically successful and includes several productions in major markets. He began in fiction and became a cult figure for THE AUDREY GREEN CHRONICLES, a series of three interlocking novels, and the epic thriller CITY OF HUMAN REMAINS. His films include UNDER THE TABLE and DESPERATE DOLLS. He has released several dozen records - from pop to noise to ambient to film soundtracks.

His website is darrencallahan.com
WIKIPEDIA is https://en.wikipedia.org/wiki/Darren_Callahan
IMDB is http://www.imdb.me/darrencallahan

Page Intentionally Left Blank

Page Intentionally Left Blank

Page Intentionally Left Blank

Page Intentionally Left Blank

Page Intentionally Left Blank

Made in the USA
Monee, IL
15 January 2024

50764488R00072